Joseph LeConte

The Race Problem in the South

Joseph LeConte

The Race Problem in the South

ISBN/EAN: 9783337001216

Printed in Europe, USA, Canada, Australia, Japan

Cover: Foto ©Suzi / pixelio.de

More available books at **www.hansebooks.com**

Evolution Series, No. 29   May 1, 1892

MAN AND THE STATE

STUDIES IN APPLIED SOCIOLOGY

LECTURES AND DISCUSSIONS BEFORE THE
BROOKLYN ETHICAL ASSOCIATION

•

"*Admirably adapted to popularize evolution views.*"—HERBERT SPENCER

Fortnightly   Ten Cents

Two Dollars and Forty Cents per annum

THE RACE PROBLEM
IN THE SOUTH

BY

PROF. JOSEPH LE CONTE, LL. D.,

President of the American Association for the Advancement of Science,
author of " Evolution as related to Religious Thought," etc.

NEW YORK
D. APPLETON AND COMPANY
1, 3, AND 5 BOND STREET
1892

EVOLUTION IN SCIENCE, PHILOSOPHY, AND ART.

A Series of Seventeen Lectures and Discussions before the Brooklyn Ethical Association. With 3 Portraits. 466 pages. 12mo. Cloth, $2.00. Separate Lectures, in pamphlet form, 10 cents each.

These popular essays, by some of the ablest exponents of the doctrine of evolution in this country, will be read with pleasure and profit by all lovers of good literature and suggestive thought. The principle of evolution, being universal, admits of a great diversity of applications and illustrations; some of those appearing in the present volume are distinctively fresh and new.

CONTENTS.

"A valuable series."—*Chicago Evening Journal.*

"The addresses include some of the most important presentations and epitomes published in America. They are all upon important subjects, are prepared with great care, and are delivered for the most part by highly eminent authorities."—*Public Opinion.*

"As a popular exposition of the latest phases of evolution this series is thorough and authoritative."—*Cincinnati Times-Star.*

New York : D. APPLETON & CO., 1, 3, & 5 Bond Street.

THE RACE PROBLEM
IN THE SOUTH

BY

JOSEPH Le CONTE, LL. D.

PRESIDENT OF THE AMERICAN ASSOCIATION FOR THE ADVANCEMENT OF SCIENCE
AUTHOR OF EVOLUTION AS RELATED TO RELIGIOUS THOUGHT, ETC.

COLLATERAL READINGS SUGGESTED:

Williams's History of the Colored Race in America; Brackett's The Negro in Maryland, and Notes on the Progress of the Colored People; Fortune's Black and White; Cable's The Negro Question, and The Silent South; Mayo's Third Estate at the South; Grady's *In Plain Black and White*, in Century, April, 1888; Bruce's The Plantation Negro as a Freeman; Blair's The Prosperity of the South Dependent on the Elevation of the Negro; Godkin's *The Republican Party and the Negro*, in Forum, May, 1889; Stetson's Problem of Negro Education; Census Statistics bearing on the Increase and Illiteracy of the Colored Race; *Statistics relating to Negro Labor in Southern Manufactures*, in Chattanooga Tradesman, 1891.

THE RACE PROBLEM IN THE SOUTH.

By Joseph Le Conte, LL. D.

Personal Relation to the Problem.

On a subject which has been discussed with so much passion and from such opposite points of view, it is absolutely necessary that one who undertakes to enlighten others should first vindicate his own right to be heard by showing his opportunities for knowing the facts at first hand, and also his ability to form an unbiased judgment. This is my excuse for bringing forward some points in my own personal history which might otherwise seem out of place.

I was born in 1823, on a large plantation near the coast of Georgia. Until approaching manhood I lived surrounded by at least two hundred blacks. In early life, therefore, I knew no other relation between whites and blacks than that of master and slave. My father managed his plantation himself, and exercised authority with firmness and kindness. The property, which had been inherited through several generations, grew by natural increase alone, none of the slaves, during my recollection, having been either bought or sold. Their moral and religious instruction, moreover, were carefully looked after. I have never known a laboring class more orderly, contented, and happy. I do not mean, however, to deny the great evils inherent in slavery, but of these I became aware only by wider experience at a later period.

With the exception of a few years spent in completing my medical and scientific education, I continued to live at the South until 1869, when I removed to California. I therefore saw and suffered the chaos of emancipation and reconstruction. Since removing to California I have several times returned and spent several months, each time, at the South. I have watched with interest the effect of emancipation on the Negro, and compared the results of slave labor and free labor.

So much for opportunities for knowing the facts. But such opportunities often prejudice the mind and incapacitate it for unbiased judgment. It is necessary, therefore, to show that, in some degree at least, I have freed myself from such prejudices.

From 1844, when I came in possession by inheritance of a portion of the property described above, until 1865, when the slaves were emancipated, at any time it would have been very greatly to my advantage to have sold out and changed the form of investment. I refused to do so only because I felt personally responsible for the welfare of the Negroes. At any time during the same interval it would have been very greatly to my advantage to have moved the property westward. I refused this also only because the Negroes were attached to the old place, and some family ties would have to be broken. Nor was my own case unique. Such sacrifice of self-interest was common in the South. It is evident, therefore, that in proportion to the conscientiousness of the owner, is this form of property a dead weight to enterprise. It is not property in the absolute sense, nor was it regarded as such. The proverbial lack of enterprise of the Old South was partly the result of the large amount of property in this form, and her conscientiousness in the treatment of it. It was to her credit that she was not more enterprising.

The catastrophe of the war and the resulting emancipation of course swept clean away everything I owned as property. The land remained—true, and still remains; but, partly on account of its situation and partly for other causes to be explained hereafter, it has never made me a cent from that day to this. Yet this total loss did not cause me any distress. On the contrary, I felt an inexpressible sense of relief and almost joy. I mention these facts to show that I had not even then any strong prejudice in favor of slavery, nor was I unprepared to welcome emancipation if it had come in the right way.

But further. Perhaps no one ever wholly frees himself from the effects of early influences and prejudices; but this much I can say with confidence: From earliest manhood, partly by reason of inherited character and partly by conscious individual effort, I have set before myself as the chief end of culture the purging of the mind of every influence that might cloud the judgment, that might dim the clearness of intellectual vision—not only on this, but on all other subjects. With this end in view, while living in New York (1843–'45), completing my medical education, and in Cambridge, Mass. (1850 and 1851), completing my scientific education, I lost no opportunity of discussing earnestly but dispassionately the subject of slavery with some of the foremost thinkers of America. It is true our subject now is not slavery; but the close connection of this question with the race problem is sufficiently evident.

The audience will pardon me the recital of these personal details. It seemed to me necessary to vindicate my right to speak at all on this subject.

Scientific Method Necessary.

Next in importance to an unbiased mind is a scientific method of treatment. There was a time when Science concerned herself only with material Nature. Questions relating to man in his higher activities, and therefore all questions of social organization, politics, ethics, etc., were regarded as hopelessly beyond her domain. The phenomena involved in these questions belonged, it was said, to a higher order, and were far too complex to be reduced to law by her methods. But meanwhile Science, laying first the foundations of rational knowledge in the simplest departments, has risen steadily higher and higher, reducing from chaos to order more and more complex subjects, until now at last she invades the very highest. Thus she passed from mathematics to mechanics, then to astronomy, then to physics, then to chemistry, reducing all to law; then, only in the present century, to biology; then, only recently, to psychology, and finally, even now, to sociology—the science of social organization and social progress, the highest of all. Again, the recent introduction of the idea of evolution by Darwin, and its extension by Spencer to every department of Nature, has revolutionized the philosophy and methods of every department of thought, especially that of sociology. It is almost needless to say, therefore, that our subject will be treated as much as possible by the scientific method, and especially in the light of the theory of evolution. The time has now come when it would seem that the further advance of civilization, and even the conservation of that which we have already achieved, is strictly conditioned on the use of more rational—i. e., of scientific—methods. This point is so fundamentally important that I stop for a moment to explain and enforce.

Art is the material embodiment of certain underlying rational principles. Science is the formal statement and discussion of these same principles. Thus art may be regarded as the embodiment or application of science. Many therefore think that science is the mother of art, and therefore must precede art. But not so. Science is rather the offspring of art. In nearly all cases art precedes science and is its condition. Levers and pulleys and inclined planes were used before the mechanical principles involved were understood. The arts of pottery, of agriculture, and of healing were practiced long before the corresponding sciences existed. Art, then, leads to science, not science to art; but when Science is sufficiently advanced she turns again and perfects art. But there is a transition stage, when an imperfect but arrogant science may interfere with the truer results of empiricism and do infinite harm. This is especially true in the more complex departments. In this stage Science ought to be strictly subordinate to a wise empiricism. She must whisper suggestions rather than utter commands. Such is the relation of science to art in agriculture and medicine to-day. To illustrate : Science is the daughter of art—heavenly daughter of an earthly mother— but when she is sufficiently grown she turns again like a good daughter and helps her mother, and even takes control of the work. But let her beware lest, in her childish vanity, her unskillful and meddlesome hands do harm instead of good.

Thus, then, there are two kinds of art—empirical art and scientific or rational art. Empirical art precedes science and is its condition ; rational art comes after science and is its embodiment. Empirical art is the outcome of the use of the intuitive reason, which works without understanding itself, and which in its highest forms we call genius. Scientific art is the outcome of the use of the formal reason which analyzes and understands the principles on which it works. Empirical art may indeed attain great perfection, but sooner or later it reaches its limit and either petrifies or decays. Scientific art, because it understands itself, is of necessity indefinitely progressive. All art, by evolution, passes through these two stages, but more slowly in proportion as the principles involved are more complex. Many arts are still in the empirical stage.

Now the highest, the most complex and difficult of all arts is the art of government—of politics, of social organization. This art, of course, preceded the science of sociology, for it is the necessary condition not only of the science of sociology but of civilization itself. This art has thus far perfected itself wholly by empirical methods. But there is one peculiarity about this art which makes advance by empirical methods irregular and doubtful. In all other arts the material is foreign to the artist; in this, artist and material are identified. Society makes itself. In this regard it is a product of evolution, not a manufactured article. But again, this evolution differs from all other kinds in this: all other evolution is by necessary law without the co-operation of the thing evolving; social evolution is mainly determined by the co-operating will of society itself. Thus it is both a product of art and of evolution. If it were the result of pure evolution by necessary law, it would be quiet and peaceful; if it were the result of pure art exercised on passive, plastic, foreign material, it would equally be peaceful. But the mingling of these two elements in varying proportion produces eternal conflict. In early stages the conflict is between classes or factions, and is violent and revolutionary; in later stages it is between parties and far less violent. But in all cases it is more or less blind, unreasoning, passionate conflict. But social evolution and the art of government have now reached a point beyond which they can not go by the use of empirical methods alone. There really seems, in this country at least, to be serious danger of retrogression in politics unless scientific methods are introduced—unless we understand the principles of sociology and try to apply them to the art of government. On the other hand, however, it is evident, from what has already been said, that the application must be made with the greatest caution and modesty, and in strict subordination to a wise empiricism. Science must be introduced into politics only as suggesting, counseling, modifying, not yet as directing and controlling. Hitherto social art has advanced in a blind, blundering, staggering way, feeling its way in the dark, retrieving its errors, recovering its falls. But now, under the light of science, even though it be yet dim, it must advance more steadily, seeing as well as feeling its way. The Ethical Association has invited discussion of political and social questions from a scientific and especially an evolution point of view. I regard this as a most hopeful sign of the times —as the beginning of a new era in politics. It is from this point of view that I desire to discuss the race problem in the South. I can not hope, of course, to solve so difficult a problem. All I can do is to lay down some scientific principles on which a solution must be based, and in all modesty to suggest some practical methods of application of these principles.

OUR BEQUEST OF SLAVERY.

No subject can be scientifically understood until studied in the light of its history. This is the historic method—the evolution method, so much used in modern research. It is necessary, therefore, first of all to give a brief outline of the history of this problem.

There was a time, and that not more than a century ago, when slavery was universally regarded as the normal, and indeed the necessary, result of the close contact of civilized with savage races. This view may be regarded as the natural one, as the survival of the law of force and the right of the strongest, inherited by man from the animal kingdom. It is doubtful whether in early stages of ethical evolution any other relation was possible or even desirable; since the only alternative would have been extinction of the weaker race. The relation of master and slave, then, is a natural one under the conditions given above. Now, let it be remembered that whatever is natural can not be wholly wrong; that the function of reason is not to despise or destroy or reverse Nature but to transform it into higher modes. But no more of this now; we will recur to it later. In any case, it will be admitted that the present century was not responsible for the existence of slavery at the South previous to the late war. It was a bequest from the previous century. Again, we must sharply distinguish between the introduction of slavery and its continuance after it was introduced. All will admit the iniquity, the incredible horror of the slave trade, but the possession and use of inherited slaves is consistent with, and may be even conducive to, the highest morality. We, therefore, say nothing more concerning the introduction of slavery into the United States. Americans were no more responsible than other civilized peoples. The South especially was, if possible, less responsible than others, for the slaves were brought not in her ships, but in those of other countries or other parts of our own country. Before the war, and the resulting emancipation, the question with the South was not as to the right or wrong of the introduction of slavery. That was a dead issue of a dead generation. "Let the dead bury their dead." The Negroes were already there; what relation must they sustain to the whites?

So, also, since the war, and consequent emancipation, the question now is not whether emancipation was right or wrong, nor, if right, whether it came in the best way. That also is a dead issue. The question now is, Being emancipated, what is best to be done with the Negro? I have called these questions dead, but they are not dead in the sense of being without living progeny. The living, in this as in all cases, has been evolved out of the dead, and must be studied in connection with the dead. This is the historic or evolution method spoken of above.

It is necessary, also, to trace briefly the history of the change of sentiment on the subject of slavery.

Immediately after the War of the Revolution all the States, unless we except Massachusetts, tolerated slavery. If slaves were more numerous in the South, it was only because the climate was more congenial and their labor more profitable there. For the same reasons there was a continual transfer of slaves from the North toward the South ; so that the disparity became greater with time. As the blacks became fewer in number, and their labor less profitable, emancipation laws were enacted in the Northern States successively. It is doubtful if the same result would have followed, at least so soon, if slaves had been more numerous and more profitable. Thus, the difference between the two sections in regard to the presence or absence of slavery was due wholly to physical causes, and not to any difference in the moral character of the people.

Now, the same was true in regard to the difference of sentiment on the subject of slavery which gradually developed in later times. It was purely the result of circumstances. Immediately after the War of Independence there was no difference of sentiment on the subject of slavery in different sections of the country. In fact, the sense of the evils of slavery, and the hope of abolishing it, seem at that time to have been stronger in Virginia and South Carolina, and other Southern States, than in the North.* But here, again, commencing from a common ground, there was a gradually increasing divergence. The same was true of many other questions closely connected with one another,

---

* Washington, Jefferson, and Madison expressed hopes of the abrogation of slavery.

Virginia, Kentucky, and Tennessee were taking steps looking toward gradual emancipation when checked by the abolition agitation.

In the first draft of the Declaration of Independence, Jefferson introduced a clause reprobating the slave trade. This was withdrawn on account of objections from some of the colonies.—Lunt, Causes of the War of '61, pp. 10–30.

and all undoubtedly contributing to the catastrophe of the war of '61. For example : Starting from a common ground, there was an increasing divergence of views on the subject of the tariff, the natural result of diversity of industries. Similarly there was an increasing divergence of views in regard to the relative claims of national and State sovereignty, the natural result of the increasing population of the Northern States, and the desire to use the national power in their own behalf. Similarly, an increasing divergence of views as to the strict or literal construction of the National Constitution, the South being ever on the defensive, and therefore strict constructionists. The same was true, and even more true, of the question of slavery. At first slavery was tolerated everywhere. Then, wherever the question could be viewed abstractly and disinterestedly, slavery was regarded as a social evil and a social danger, but no longer avoidable. We must make the best of it. Then the sentiment of the world against it became ever stronger, and it was regarded as not only a social but a moral evil—what at all hazards ought to be removed. Then it became a mortal sin, then a crime, then the sum of all crimes ! Then, of course, there commenced a holy crusade against it.

In the mean time a contrary movement of sentiment was going on at the South. As slave labor became more and more profitable, chiefly by the increasing culture of cotton and rice, which, more than any other products, require the control of labor; as the number of slaves became greater and greater, partly by congeniality of climate, partly by migration from the North, but chiefly by the better care of the slaves and their increased reproduction— the emancipation of the slaves became more and more difficult, partly on account of the enormous amount of property in this form, but especially on account of the extremely grave social question involved. Now, as emancipation seemed more and more impossible, slavery more and more fixed, the South, as was natural, set herself to finding some rational grounds for the defense of slavery, and many even persuaded themselves that, instead of a curse, it was a blessing, and even the sum of all blessings.

But, in spite of these attempts to defend and even to apotheosize slavery, in the minds of thinking men there was an uneasy and even painful sense of isolation from the rest of the civilized world and a consequent stagnation of the current of progress. It was easily perceived that in many ways slavery was a blight on the prosperity of the South. Thirty years before the war the South was fully abreast of the foremost of the Northern States in enterprise, both commercial and manufacturing, in literature and in art, and, in fact, in all that constitutes a vigorous progressive civilization. But these thirty years were years of complete revolution in the world's sentiment on the subject of slavery. They were also years of prodigious advance everywhere except in the South. She stood still while the rest of the world rushed on. That the cause of this was slavery there could be no doubt. No people can with impunity cut itself off from sympathy with the rest of the civilized world. It must be left behind in the race. Civilization is no longer national, nor even racial. It must be human.

Such was the condition of things in 1861. Such is a brief history of the growth of the "irrepressible conflict" between the North and the South. I will not stop to discuss the causes of the war. Others can do this better than I; and, besides, that is not the subject now in hand. Certain it is, however, that it was the natural result of increasing divergence of interests and sentiment on many subjects already mentioned, until finally parties became essentially sectional. Undoubtedly, however, by far the most fundamental of these, and perhaps the determining cause of all the other divergences, was the question of slavery. But still more fundamental than this—than all these—in fact, the underlying cause of all revolutions—is the irrational, unscientific, empirical methods of politics, already described. If revolutions are to be prevented in future, it must be by the use of more rational methods, by understanding the laws of sociology, and the wise application of these laws in politics.

OF SLAVES AS PROPERTY.

I have already spoken of the overwhelming loss of property suffered by the South as the result of the war and consequent emancipation. This leads me to say something on the economic question of slaves as property. Let it be understood, however, that what I say on this subject is the result of my own thoughts only, and carries no authority with it except its reasonableness. I do not profess to be a political economist. It may be that the views I am about to express are those of political economists generally, but I am sure they are not usually held by intelligent people.

When the war was ended and emancipation accepted, everybody regarded the situation at the South as that of so many thousand million dollars' worth of property completely annihilated, gone out of existence like that which takes place in the burning of a house. Now this, I am convinced, is not true. I well remember at that time astounding some of my friends by asserting that, under favorable conditions and a due relation between the amount of land and slaves, there would be no loss at all, but only a change of form of labor. I illustrated this then, and I would illustrate it now, as follows: Suppose I own a certain amount of land, and slaves enough to work it; obviously the value of the whole property would be determined by the resulting average income. But it will be admitted, and subsequent events have proved, that the same land worked faithfully by free hired labor would make fully as much income. Evidently, then, the value of the property would be unchanged; the value of the land alone after emancipation would be equal to the value of land and slaves before. In other words, the whole value of the slaves would be transferred bodily over to the land. I repeat, then, that if after emancipation the Negroes had continued to work faithfully for wages, the products of the land would have been undiminished, and therefore there would have been no perceptible loss of property at all. The great loss of property and the awful prostration of the South was wholly the result of the complete disorganization of the labor system. An old system had been destroyed, the new had not yet been established. The whole trouble was the unfortunate suddenness of the change and the time necessary for readjustment. It is impossible on any other view to account for the rapid recuperation of the South. In many places, it is true, the recuperation was slow; in some places the recuperation has not taken place at all; but this is only because the reorganization of labor has been slower or has not taken place at all. This is the case, for example, on the coast of Georgia already mentioned, and in many other places. The number of blacks in these places is too great to feel the influence of the whites. The community is essentially African, and therefore with little or no ambition to improve. Living is easy with even a minimum of labor. The Negroes are unwilling to work for wages. The whites in despair have mostly moved away and abandoned the cultivation of their lands. On this view it is easy to account for individual cases of utter loss—of reduction from affluence to abject poverty. But such cases are exceptions.

It is evident, then, that slaves are not property at all in the sense that other things are property. They are not, and never were, regarded at the South as mere chattels, though doubtless too much so in many cases. Slavery is only the right, or at least the power, to control labor. Wherever capital controls labor there is slavery. If slave labor in any case is more profitable than free labor, it is only because it is more controllable.

ETHNOLOGICAL ASPECTS OF THE PROBLEM.

Under this general head come several questions of fundamental importance. Among these I discuss, first—

(a) *The Laws of the Effects of Race Contact.*

The laws determining the effects of contact of species, races, varieties, etc., among animals may be summed up under the formula, "The struggle for life and the survival of the fittest." It is vain to deny that the same law is applicable to the races of man also. All the factors of organic evolution are carried forward into human evolution, only they are modified by an additional and higher factor, Reason, in proportion to the dominance of that factor—i. e., in proportion to civilization. In organic evolution the contact of two diverse forms determines either the extinction of the weaker or else its relegation to a subordinate place in the economy of Nature; the weaker is either destroyed or seeks safety by avoiding competition. In human evolution the same law must hold, with a difference to be determined by reason. At the outset of this discussion, therefore, it is necessary to lay down a fundamental proposition which must underlie all our reasonings on this subject : Given two races widely diverse in intellectual and moral elevation, and especially in capacity for self-government—i. e., in grade of race evolution ; place them together in equal numbers and under such conditions that they can not get away from one another, and leave them to work out for themselves as best they can the problem of social organization, and the inevitable result will be, must be, ought to be, that the higher race will assume control and determine the policy of the community. Not only is this result inevitable, but it is the best result for both races, especially for the lower race.

To illustrate: Suppose there be cast on a desert island 100 grown-up people and 100 children of, say, ten years old, but having no blood relationship the one set with the other, and a community be there organized. Is it not inevitable—is it not best for all parties, but especially for the children—that the grown-up people should assume entire control and determine the policy of the community, while the children should be subordinated to their authority? Is not this just, is it not right? Talk about violation of the rights of the weaker! The sacredest of all rights, because the right most apt to be violated, is the right of the weak and the ignorant to the control and guidance of the strong and the wise. Would not even compulsory service in proportion to ability and in return for protection and guidance be better than neglect and consequent extermination?

Or suppose 1,000 Anglo-Saxons and the same number of Australian blacks be put together in the same place and surrounded by an unscalable wall so that they could not run away from the experiment. Is it not evident that the founding of a civilized community is strictly conditioned on the complete supremacy of the white race? The disparity between the two classes in this case is fully as great as in the last, but the problem would be far more difficult, because of the physical strength and animal ferocity of the Australian as compared with the physical weakness, and especially the docility, of the children. But in some way—peaceable if possible, forcible if necessary—the higher race must control and determine the policy of the community. Here again even compulsory service, if necessary, in proportion to ability and in return for protection and guidance, is best for both races, but especially for the lower race; for the only alternative for them is extermination. You may call it slavery if you like. If so, then slavery under certain conditions is right. But the relation, if kindly and wisely administered, is not slavery in any philosophic sense.

We have said above that the inevitable result of such contact is either subordination of some kind or degree, or else extermination. Which it will be, depends on the character of the two races, especially the lower. If it be in the early stages of race-evolution, and therefore plastic, docile, imitative, some form of subordination will be the result; if, on the other hand, it be highly specialized and rigid, extermination is unavoidable. The Negro is probably the best type of the former and the American Indian of the latter.

Now, the condition of things at the South to-day, though certainly not identical, is similar to that described above. Here we have two races widely different in grade of evolution, in nearly equal numbers in the same place. The difference in grade may not be as great as that described above: but, if not, we owe it to the previous condition of subordination to the white race. The result, therefore, must be similar, though certainly not identical with the cases described above. As a broad general fact, control of some kind or degree must be in the hands of the superior race. I do not say that the best form of such control is slavery. If it ever were the best form (as it probably once was), it is not so now. The Negro under slavery, and by means of slavery (for in no other way was close and peaceable contact of the two races possible), has been developed above slavery. Slavery was probably at one time the only natural or even possible relation between the two races, and was therefore right. The evils were not in the institution, but in its abuses. But by race-evolution of the Negro this relation became less and less natural, and therefore less and less right. It was probably becoming wrong before the war. Even without a war, and an emancipation proclamation, I believe slavery would certainly have come to an end, not by the external pressure of a foreign sentiment, but by the internal pressure of race-growth. The race-evolution of the Negro had gone as far as it was possible under the conditions of slavery. Freedom in some form or degree was necessary for its further evolution. I say "some form or degree"; for the right to freedom, as we understand it in this country, has not yet been achieved by the Negro race in the South, as a whole. By slavery the Negro has been educated up to the right to some measure of freedom, but not as a race to complete freedom. Some form or degree of control by the white race is still absolutely necessary. I mean not personal control, but control of State policy. There can be no doubt that some device by means of which the policy of the community shall be substantially under the control of those alone who are most capable of self-government is the absolute condition of civilization there. What is the best legal device for this purpose is just the problem to be worked out by the Southern people, and they will work it out if let alone.

The Wide Significance of the Problem.

It is impossible to exaggerate the importance to the South of this problem, for the very existence of a civilized community there is conditioned on its successful solution. But it is also a problem of widest application, affecting all the races on the face of the earth. Everywhere the white race is pushing its way among lower races. Everywhere, now that slavery is inadmissible, the result is gradual extinction of the lower race. And this tendency to destroy lower races is steadily increasing with the increased energy of modern civilization. Is this result inevitable? If not, how is it to be avoided? Nowhere are the opportunities for the successful solution of this question so favorable as at the South to-day. In the first place, the problem is a more pressing one there than anywhere else; it must be solved, and that speedily. In the second place, the Negro is the very best race that could be selected for the purpose. As this is an important point, I stop a moment to explain.

In this regard the inferior races may be divided into two groups—viz., those which are inferior because undeveloped, and those which are so because developed, perhaps highly developed, in a limited way or in a wrong direction. Races of the first group may be called generalized; they are plastic, adaptable to new conditions, and therefore easily molded by contact with higher races. Those of the second group are specialized; they are rigid, unadaptable to new conditions. The Negro is the best type of the first group, and perhaps the Chinese of the second group. The Chinese are a highly developed race, but extremely rigid under the influence of other races. The Japanese are far more plastic. The Negro has many fine and hopeful qualities. He is plastic, docile, impressionable, sympathetic, imitative, and therefore in a high degree improvable by contact with a superior race and under suitable conditions. It is doubtful if any other race could have so thrived and improved under slavery as the Negro has done. But, although the Negro by means of slavery has been raised above slavery, it would be a great mistake to suppose that he has yet reached the position of equality with the white race—that unassisted he can found a free civilized community. The question, therefore, still remains, What is the just and rational relation that should subsist between the two races? It is the problem of race-contact everywhere, but here under conditions most favorable for successful solution.

Objections.

Doubtless many objections will be raised against the foregoing positions. Many persons will not even admit the gravity of the problem, or that any solution is necessary. For them, the formula, " All men are born equal," is a sufficient solution. They say that the Southern people are wholly wrong in imagining any difficulty in the matter—that elsewhere among civilized peoples, as, for example, in Europe and in New England, Negroes are treated much like people of other and whiter color. True; but it must be borne in mind that relative numbers' is a prime factor in the question. If there be only a few of a lower race scattered about in a community, we can afford to recognize, nay more, to patronize—nay more, if it serves any purpose, to lionize them. But when the numbers are equal or nearly so, when there is a struggle between the two races for control of the policy of the community, the case is very different. The higher race must take control. There is not a civilized community in the world that would not demand this. The Hindu visitor in England is treated with respect, and even lionized, but in India the race line is drawn nearly as sharply as it is at the South, and yet the Hindu is a Caucasian—aye, even an Aryan people. See, again, the relation between the English and the aboriginal Australian or the New Zealander whenever they come in close contact. If the problem is not so serious in these countries, it is only because there is still room enough and to spare—the lower race may withdraw itself from close contact, if it so desires. It is evident, then, that the feeling which draws the race line is not peculiar to the South, but is found everywhere under similar conditions. Nor is it a matter of political party. Northern Republicans, settling at the South, soon catch the infection.

But it will be objected again that any relation between the races other than that of complete equality in all respects is manifestly in conflict with the fundamental law of the nation, and especially the recent amendments of the Constitution. I sincerely hope not. I hope and believe that there may be found some just and rational method of solving this problem which will not be in conflict with

2

fundamental law. But if not—if there be indeed a radi-
cal discordance, an irreconcilable conflict between fundamental law and the position taken above—then I do not
hesitate to say, So much the worse for the fundamental law
and the constitutional amendments, for it only shows that
these are themselves in conflict with the still more fundamental laws of Nature, which are the laws of God. If it be
so, then the South is very sorry, but it can't be helped.
There is a law of self-preservation for communities as well
as for individuals, and this law takes precedence of all other
laws. It is a higher law if you like. It will be remembered
that in 1850 Massachusetts, too, preached a higher law than
the Constitution. If ever there were a case in which the
doctrine of a higher law was justifiable, surely it is this. It
is true that sacrifice of the individual freely to the State is
noble. It is true that Socrates—not to mention a still
higher and diviner example—subordinated the law of self-
preservation itself to the laws of the State, and we reverence
him for so doing. But remember, first, that this was done
on high ethical, not legal, grounds; and, secondly, that
when, as in this case, the question is that of preservation,
not of the individual, but of the community, of civilization,
of the interests of humanity, the law of self-preservation
stands on the highest ethical as well as the strictest legal
grounds. In this case the right of self-preservation becomes
the duty of self-preservation.

The whites, I believe, desire earnestly—more earnestly than
can be well imagined by those at a distance—the real best
interests of the blacks. They earnestly desire their elevation
both by education and by acquisition of property. There can
be no better evidence of this than the fact that nearly the
whole expense (ninety per cent in South Carolina) of the
education of the blacks is borne by the whites. They would
grant, I am sure, every just right; but all on the one condition that in some way the whites shall, for the present at
least, substantially control the policy of the State. This is
an absolute necessity at present and until some better solution of the problem be devised, until some better line than
the race-line be drawn between the capables and the
incapables. That this is true is plainly shown by the disastrous results of the brief reign of carpet-baggers sustained
by Negro votes after the war, and the immediate restoration
of order and prosperity so soon as the whites again assumed
control.

But it will be objected again that the race-line is artificial, and therefore unjust and irrational, and that there are many blacks more capable of intelligently directing the policy of the State than some whites. Yes, this is true. But are not all lines more or less artificial? Can there be anything more artificial than the age-line? Are there not many persons under twenty-one more capable than many over twenty-one? In this case, it is true, the admitted injustice will be speedily removed by advancing age. But so in the other, also, the admitted injustice will, we hope, be removed, though not so speedily, by race-growth, race-education. In both cases it is an age-line—in the one case of the individual, in the other of the race. The one is no more unjust than the other.

But again it will be objected that the race-line is wholly the result of race-prejudice, and this in its turn only a remnant of slavery. It may, indeed, be partly the result of race-prejudice, but not, I think, a remnant of slavery. The race-prejudice is not confined to the South. On the contrary, it is probably less there than elsewhere. But race-prejudice or race-repulsion, to use a stronger term, is itself not a wholly irrational feeling. It is probably an instinct necessary to preserve the blood purity of the higher race. But of this I shall have more to say hereafter.

(b) *The Principles of Race-improvement.*

I have spoken of the color-line as a race-age-line, which, even though no better line could be drawn, would not remain, but be eventually removed by race-development. This leads me to speak of the principles of race-improvement.

It has been imagined by many over-sanguine persons that the whole race problem will be speedily solved by public-school education. This, I suppose, is the form of solution present in the minds of most people. I am quite sure this is to some extent a delusion. Education has done much for the Negro, but it will not solve the problem in this generation, nor in many generations. The education of the individuals must not be confounded with the evolution of the race. There can be no doubt that the evolution of races is largely determined by the same factors that determine the evolution of the organic kingdom. Now, there are some biologists of highest rank who go so far as to deny that individual acquirements can be inherited at all. If these biologists are right, then education of individuals does not improve the race at all. I do not agree with these biologists, and have given my reasons in a previous article.* Nevertheless, it is certain that in animals, and also in man, the whole improvement of the individual is not carried over bodily into the next generation by inheritance, but only a very small part. A small part of the improvement of each generation is carried over by inheritance to the next, and this, accumulating from age to age, constitutes the gradual evolution of the race. Thus the education of the individual is one thing and the evolution of the race is another and very different thing. The one is a question of a few years, the other a question of centuries, perhaps millenniums. The truth is, education—i. e., school education, book education—is usually regarded as a panacea for all the evils of society. But this is a false and very pernicious view. The experimental philosophy of the last age, and still ʼprevalent in this, would make the whole intellectual and moral capital of every individual the result of his own individual acquirement. This is an arrogant philosophy. It exalts too much the importance of the individual, and has had much to do with many of the evils of society of the present day. But one of the most important recent modifications of our philosophy of life, forced upon us by the theory of evolution, is the recognition of the fact that a very large part of every man's intellectual and moral capital comes by inheritance. In animals all or nearly all is inherited; in man a part is inherited and a part individually acquired. The higher the race, the larger is the proportion of individual acquirement. But in all cases the inherited bank account is continually growing from generation to generation by small additions from individual acquisition. The growing inheritance constitutes the evolution of the race.

But some will object that, so far as the evidence of the schools is concerned, there is no sufficient reason for regarding the Negro as at all lower than the white race. On the contrary, the Negro pupils show remarkable brightness. This is probably true. They do indeed show brightness, quickness of memory, keenness of senses, precocity of perceptive faculties. These qualities are very characteristic of nearly all lower races (and, indeed, also of animals); but they must not be confounded with the reflective, originating,

* The Factors of Evolution, etc. The Monist for July, 1891.

rational faculties which develop late, and show themselves in active life rather than in school. It is in these highest faculties alone that the great difference exists.

Again : In these modern times there is a strong tendency to exaggerate the importance of *formal* education (i.e., school education, book education) as compared with *informal* education. Now, in all of us, but especially in lower races, it is the informal education—that which comes by contact with higher individuals and higher races—that is by far the most important in the formation of character, and therefore for self-government and fitting for citizenship. The simple contact with the white race in slavery times, and the same contact together with the necessity of self-support since emancipation, has done more for the elevation of the Negro than school education alone could possibly have done. Not only has the Negro been elevated to his present condition by contact with the white race, but he is sustained in that position wholly by the same contact, and whenever that support is withdrawn he relapses again to his primitive state. The Negro race is still in childhood ; it has not yet learned to walk alone in the paths of civilization. In the South to-day wherever the whites predominate, so that the policy of the community is determined by them alone, the Negroes are industrious, thrifty, commencing to acquire property, and, in fact, improving in every way. But, on the contrary, wherever the Negroes are largely in excess, as in some portions of the coast regions of the South Atlantic and Gulf States, so that the influence of the whites is scarcely felt and the community is essentially African, the Negroes are rapidly falling back into savagery, and even resuming many of their original pagan rites and superstitions.

(c) Principles of Race-mixture.

Another proposed solution of the problem is complete race-mixture. Race-mixture often produces good effects : why not this? I know of no American writer of distinction who has proposed this solution, but some thoughtful English writers see no other solution possible. This brings me to discuss this subject in the light of biology, and especially of evolution.

In a previous article, on Genesis of Sex (Popular Science Monthly, November, 1879), I have treated this subject more fully on the biological side, and in another article, on Mixture of Races (Berkeley Quarterly for April, 1880), I have applied the biological principles to the subject of human progress. I can here only give a brief *résumé*, referring the reader for fuller details to the articles mentioned.

Darwin, by abundant and conclusive experiments, has shown that in plants in which the flowers are bisexual—i. e., contain both stamens and pistils—and are thus self-fertilizing, if self-fertilization be prevented and cross-fertilization between different flowers of the same plant, or, still better, between flowers of different plants of the same species, be effected, the result will be more and larger seeds, and therefore more and healthier offspring, than in the case of self-fertilization. Now, this experiment undoubtedly furnishes the key to the explanation of the advantages of sexual over other forms of generation, and the object of its introduction, as well as of much else in the process of evolution. There can be no doubt that non-sexual preceded sexual modes of generation, and that the sexual modes were introduced in order thereby to bring about cross-fertilization; and, furthermore, that throughout the whole evolution of the organic kingdom the constant effort of Nature has been to bring about an increasing diversity of the crossing individuals up to a limit which will be presently explained; and, finally, that the object of all this, or at least its effect, has been to produce better and better results in the offspring.

The steps of this process were briefly as follows: (1) First there was only the simplest conceivable form of generation, viz., that by fission—fissiparous generation. Here there is not even the distinction between parent and offspring. (2) Next there was generation by budding—gemmiparous generation—but from any part alike. Here first emerges the distinction of parent and offspring, for the bud is but a small part of the original organism. (3) Then, by the law of specialization, the function of budding is relegated to a particular part, and we have a budding organ. (4) Then by another general law the budding organ is transferred for greater safety to an interior surface, and thus simulates an ovary, though not a true ovary. (5) Then this organ develops two kinds of cells—sperm-cell and germ-cell. Here for the first time we have the sexual elements—male and female—which by their union produce the ovum, which in its turn develops into the offspring. This is the lowest form of sexual generation. We have male and female *elements*, but not male and female *organs*, much less male and female *individuals*. (6) The next step is the separation of the two organs, male and female—spermary and ovary—which prepare the two elements, sperm-cell and germ-cell; but these organs yet remain in the same individual. This is hermaphroditism, almost universal among plants and very common among lower animals. (7) The next step is the introduction of devices of many kinds to prevent self-fertilization and insure cross-fertilization between different hermaphroditic individuals. (8) The next step is the separation of the sexual organs in different individuals, thus entirely preventing self-fertilization; and the introduction of sex-attraction, insuring cross-fertilization. (9) The next step is the gradually increasing diversity of the crossing individuals—i. e., of the males and females. (10) The last step, and the one which specially concerns us here, is the crossing of males and females of different varieties of the same species. These are the principal steps; but of course there are many gradations between.

Now, the effect, and therefore the object, of this whole process of gradual differentiation is the bringing about of better results in the offspring. Why the results are better, is more obscure. It is undoubtedly due in some way to the increasing diversity of the qualities inherited by the offspring from the two parents—the funding of diverse qualities in a common offspring. This may improve the offspring in two ways: First, by the struggle for life among the many qualities, good and bad, strong and weak, inherited from both sides, and the survival of the strongest and best qualities. Secondly, diversity of inheritance tends to variation of offspring, and this furnishes materials for natural selection, and thus hastens the process of evolution. But *there is a limit to the good effects of this differentiation of uniting individuals;* for the union of individuals of different species is either less fertile or wholly infertile. In other words, when the difference between the uniting individuals reaches the extent which we call species, then Nature practically forbids the bans. I say *practically* forbids. There are many degrees of fertility and infertility between species. In most cases the infertility is absolute—i. e., the union is without offspring. In some there is offspring, but the offspring is a sterile hybrid which dies without issue. In some the hybrid is fertile, but its offspring is feeble, and therefore quickly eliminated in the struggle for life with the pure stock, and becomes extinct in a few generations; or else it is more fertile with the pure stock than with other hybrids, and therefore is absorbed into one or other of the parent stocks, and the original species remain distinct. If this were not so, there would be no such thing as species at all.

Now, to sum up and apply: It is well known that in the higher animals close, consanguineous, in-and-in breeding continued for a long time weakens the stock, while judicious crossing of varieties strengthens the stock. But there must be a limit beyond which the effect again becomes bad; for when the difference between the uniting individuals reaches the extent of species, Nature forbids the bans—i. e., there is no result at all. It is evident, therefore, that we may represent the effect of cross-breeding among higher animals by a sinuous curve, as shown below:

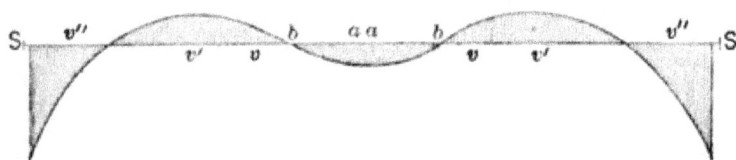

DIAGRAM ILLUSTRATING THE EFFECTS OF CROSS-BREEDING.

In this diagram the horizontal line represents the average results of indiscriminate breeding, or the ordinary typical condition of the species. Distance of points on this line represents the amount of difference of uniting individuals, and the sinuous line represents the varying effects of crossing of selected varieties. Where this line passes below the horizontal line it shows effects below the average; when above that line, effects above the average. By inspection it is seen that close in-and-in breeding, *a a*, produces bad effects; *b b* represent ordinary individual differences, the crossing of which produces average results, and tends to maintain the average level; *v v* represent varieties, the crossing of which produces good results, which rise to a maximum at *v' v'*, and then declining again, become bad or below the average at *v'' v''*; until, finally, when the difference of the uniting individuals reaches the extent which we call species, *s s*, then the result becomes infinitely bad—i. e., produces no offspring. In a general way, therefore, the diagram represents the facts of cross-breeding.

Now, there can be no doubt that the above law applies also to man, with perhaps some modifications, to be determined by investigation. There can be no doubt that long-continued consanguineous, in-and-in breeding has a bad effect also in man, and probably even more so than in animals. I am well aware that some recent writers have contested this statement, but the examples cited are those of isolated communities under peculiarly healthy conditions; and, moreover, the argument relates only to the physical and not to the psychical nature. But it is the psychical nature which is peculiarly sensitive, and which we are specially concerned with here, for we are discussing the effects on human evolution or progress. Bodily health and strength are, of course, a necessary underlying condition; but human evolution is spiritual, not bodily. Organic evolution is by change of form and making of new species, in order to come into harmony with an ever-changing environment. Man, on the other hand, changes the environment so as to bring it into harmony with himself and his wants; and, therefore, his evolution is not by change of form or making of new species of man, but by change of character and elevation of the plane of his activity.

But to return. There can be no doubt that consanguineous breeding of families, true breeding in isolated communities, and even continuous breeding within the limits of a national variety, tend in various degrees to fixedness of character, customs, laws, modes of thought and feeling, and thus, finally, to rigidity and arrest of development; while, on the other hand, the crossing of family bloods, communal bloods, and national bloods tends not only to strengthen physically and mentally by the survival of the best qualities inherited from both sides, but also, and much more, to prevent fixedness of character and arrest of development, to confer plasticity, comprehensiveness, many-sidedness, and thus to promote progress. No doubt commerce, travel, education, all tend in the same direction, but mixture of blood and diverse inheritance is the most direct and potent means of accomplishing this result.

It is evident, then, that the effect of mixing human varieties is similar to the effect of mixing animal varieties, and that in a general way both are truly represented by the diagram. The only question that remains is: What amount of difference produces maximum results; and where, if anywhere, do bad results begin? This question can not be answered with certainty; but it seems probable that the crossing of national varieties, and perhaps of all varieties within the limits of the four or five primary races, may produce good effects; but that the crossing of these primary races themselves produces bad effects. It seems probable that in the evolution of man from the animal kingdom there was a differentiation into varieties so strong that they may be regarded as incipient species. If so, then the divergence between these primary races has passed the limit within which crossing has a good effect. The results of such crossing partake somewhat of the nature of hybrids— they are less strong than either of the pure races. Race-aversion—which certainly exists, though it may be overleaped by passion—is probably a sign of a difference approaching specific.

This conclusion, reached by general considerations alone, is substantially confirmed by such loose observations as have been made on such crosses. Opportunities of widest observation on this point occur at the South; but, unfortunately, they have not been as careful and scientific as we would desire. There seems little doubt, however, that mulattoes have not the strength and endurance of either of the pure races. It is certain that they are much more liable to hereditary diseases, especially the different forms of scrofula. It is almost certain that when they marry among themselves the next generation is even still feebler; and it is probable, though not certain, that in a few generations they would die out unless re-enforced by the stronger blood of the pure races, in which case, of course, they would disappear by absorption into the one race or the other. In intellect the mulatto is certainly superior to the Negro; but it is doubtful if he attains even the mean between the two races; it is doubtful whether the white blood does not lose more than the black gains by the mixture. These conclusions have been reached by nearly all observers, as, for example, by Morton, Nott, Glidden, Gobineau, Ferrier, etc. I know of but one writer—Quatrefages—who contests them. The question is a very complex one. Moral influences may have much to do with the dying out of a race. The anomalous position of the mulatto, recognized by neither race, may have its effect. But this again is only another evidence that successful mixing is impossible.

But some, even here in America, have thought that, whether we like it or not, whether the effect of mixture be good or bad, the problem is going to solve itself in this way. I am not sure, but I think they are mistaken. The mixing of the races has been greatly exaggerated because observed mostly in the cities. On the plantations the mixed breeds have always been rare. In the next place, the mixing is becoming less and less every day. In proportion as the Negroes become more self-respecting, they withdraw more and more from this kind of relation with the whites, and to some extent from the mixed breeds. The mixed breeds are not increasing in number, and, as already said, they will either die out or be absorbed into one or other of the pure races. In addition to this natural and spontaneous withdrawal, nearly if not quite all of the Southern States have passed laws forbidding mixed marriages. In this regard, therefore, the color-line is likely to be permanent.*

DESTINY OF THE LOWER RACES.

The extreme interest of the general question of the destiny of the lower races, and its close connection with the question in hand, induces me to digress here in order to discuss it very briefly.

If the views presented above be true, then for the lower races everywhere (leaving out slavery) there is eventually but one of two alternatives—viz., either extermination or mixture. But if mixture makes a feeble race, then this also is only a slower process of extermination. Is extermination, then, the inexorable fate of all the lower races? Shall the pitiless law of organic evolution—the law of destruction of the weak and the survival of only the strongest races—be the law of human evolution also? It may indeed be so, but let us hope not. It may be that there is a way of escape. Let us see.

I suppose the blue-eyed, fair-haired Teuton on the one hand, and the black on the other, may be regarded as extreme types, and that their mixture will produce the worst results. The mixture of the Spaniard and Indian in Mexico and South America has produced a hardy and prolific race, although it must be acknowledged that the result in social

* Some years ago it was believed and stated that the blacks were increasing much faster than the whites. If this were true, they would soon overrun not only the South, but the whole country. But it is not true. The belief was based on false statistics which are now corrected. The problem is serious enough without this aggravation. They are not now increasing as fast as the whites, on account of the much higher death-rate.

organization and social progress has not been encouraging.
But if we admit the result in this case as more favorable
than that in the case of the mixture of the Anglo-Saxon
and the Negro, may we not in this fact glimpse a hope for
the lower races in general ? The primary races, though wide
apart in their extreme types, approach each other on their
margins. Is it not possible that these marginal varieties
of primary races may approach sufficiently near to mix with
advantage, and thus may be formed secondary types that
may mix successfully with even the extreme types? To
illustrate : If the connection between the extreme types
form an arch too wide to be stable, may not each extreme
connect with a more intermediate type on each side, and
form two stable arches which shall be the abutments of a
still higher central arch? If mixing is possible at all, it
would seem that it must be by such gradual approaches.

Now, there are many reasons for believing that if successful mixing be at all possible, such mixing would be better
for humanity than extinction of the lower races and the
survival of the white race alone. There are valuable qualities in the lower races which ought not to be lost, which
ought to be incorporated into the perfect ideal humanity
for which we hope; and this can be done only, or at least
most directly, by mixture. The effect of true breeding as
already seen may be excellent in one direction—i. e., in per-
fecting certain limited qualities—but tends to fix and finally
to petrify character and arrest progress. Mixing produces
a more plastic material, a better clay, a more generalized and
therefore a more progressive type. Therefore it may well
be that, after the best results of breeding within the limits
of the primary races have been attained in the production
of the highest race civilizations in several directions, then
the judicious mixture, as explained above, of these perfected
varieties, will produce a generalized type capable of indefinite progress in *all* directions. Civilization, then, will
no longer be Anglo-Saxon, or Teutonic, or European, or
Aryan, or Caucasian, but human. If something like this
be not possible, then are the lower races indeed doomed.

Or, to put it another way : Any civilization is long-lived
in proportion as it is general—i. e., as it includes more of
the elements of a complete humanity. Greek civilization
was admirable, but simple, narrow, national. Therefore,
like an annual plant, it grew up rapidly, flowered and fruited
gloriously, and died quickly. Roman civilization was more

general. It was not national but Mediterranean. It was longer-lived—its trunk more solid but not perennial. It also perished. Modern civilization is Aryan. It is still more general, more complex, contains more elements of humanity, and is therefore still longer-lived. But unless it incorporates *all* the elements of a perfect humanity, it also must perish. If there be indeed valuable qualities in the lower races and characteristic of them which ought to be incorporated in a perfect humanity, then the ideal civilization must include these also. The final civilization will thus be coextensive with human nature, with the earth surface, and with the life of humanity.

After this digression on the general question of the destiny of the lower races, we return to the immediate subject in hand—viz., the adjustment, in the light of the preceding principles, of the relation between the two races in the South on a just and rational basis. On this strictly practical subject I shall be brief, because my main object is the exposition of principles, not their application in practical politics. If the question be only viewed in the right spirit and from the scientific standpoint, it will be quickly solved by practical men.

The problem divides itself into two main branches—viz., the political and the ethical. The political is the more immediate and urgent, and therefore taken up first; but the ethical is more fundamental.

THE POLITICAL PROBLEM.

Before taking up any special mode of solution, it is necessary to insist on an important general principle. The race problem, like all complex social problems, is not to be solved at once out of hand, as many think. We have had far too much of this kind of solution of political problems already in history. A true solution is a slow process of evolution, having many steps, each adapted to the existing conditions. The final solution is only reached in an ideal condition of society. This is what is meant by a question solving itself. The only question at any moment is: What is the best thing to be done now under present conditions? The problem is a complex equation, requiring many steps in its solution. The question is, What is the best next step?

Some imagine that all that is necessary to solve the problem is to break up the "solid South"—that parties should divide as elsewhere on other lines than the color-line. This, like many other pretended solutions, is a mere ignoring of the problem. Eventually, doubtless, parties must so divide, but not now, nor until some other or better line between the capables and the incapables be drawn and recognized. The Negro race as a whole is certainly at present incapable of self-government and unworthy of the ballot; and their participation without distinction in public affairs can only result in disaster. The Negroes themselves are beginning to recognize this. They are withdrawing themselves more and more from politics. Everywhere the black vote is small in proportion to their numbers. And this is due not wholly to intimidation, as many think. Doubtless intimidation has been used in the South as elsewhere; perhaps more than elsewhere, for the motive was stronger—viz., the existence of a civilized community. But this is not the only nor indeed the principal cause. The Negroes now see that their first hopes of the magical power of the ballot were fallacious. They are now beginning to believe that the whites are not their enemies but their friends, and are better able to take care of their interests than they are themselves. Thus, even in the sea-coast counties of Georgia, which I have recently visited, where the blacks outnumber the whites in some parts ten to one, and where intimidation is impossible and never was attempted, the county is now represented in the Legislature by white men alone. The same thing is shown by the fact that the law making the payment of a poll-tax of one or two dollars a qualification for voting practically disfranchises nearly all the blacks; not because they can not pay it, but because to them the privilege is not worth so much.

I repeat, then, that the blacks as a whole are unworthy of the ballot. The South is not solid against the North or against any party as a party, but she is solid for self-government by the white race as the only self-governing race. Until some better line be drawn defining a self-governing class, she is obliged to be solid. That some such better line will be made I can not doubt, for the color-line pure and simple can not continue. It is not only manifestly unjust, and therefore debauching to the political honesty of the whites, but is a constant source of irritation, and therefore fraught with danger.

But the question returns: By what just and legal means can we secure government by a self-governing class alone?

I answer without hesitation: By a limitation of the ballot, by a qualification for voting, both of education and of property. I see no possible solution but this, and this I believe would be effectual. It would be perfectly just and perfectly rational. It would exclude many whites, but only such as should be excluded. It would include many blacks, but only such as are fit to vote. I said a qualification both of education and of property. Perhaps most persons will agree to the justice of the former; but I regard the latter as by far the more important. It is so not only nor mainly on the ground usually assigned—viz., its conservative tendency—but also and chiefly because it is the best index of a self-governing capacity. In the higher races, in advanced stages of civilization, and in highly cultured communities there are doubtless many men who take no heed to accumulate property, not, however, from shiftlessness, but because they have higher and better things to do. They are so busy with higher and better things that they have no time to make money. But in uncultured men generally, and especially in lower races, there is no better, I might almost say there is no other, evidence of character necessary for the exercise of the ballot than the steady industry and self-denial necessary to accumulate property. Mere book education, on the contrary, though easily acquired by the Negro on account of his quick apprehensiveness, has little effect on character, and is but small guarantee for self-governing capacity.

I would make the qualification of both kinds small—as small as is at all consistent with effectiveness—because I recognize the powerfully educating effect of the ballot itself. Freedom educates for freedom, and therefore should be given even in larger measure than deserved. Privilege educates for the right use of privilege, and therefore as much should be given as is consistent with safety. This is a true principle in all education, whether of individuals, of communities, or of races. But although the ballot educates for the right use of the ballot, yet its reasonable limitation is a still more potent educator; for it is the most powerful of all inducements to improvement of all kinds.

The golden opportunity for the introduction of these qualifications was certainly at the time of the reconstruction of the Southern States immediately after the war. I well remember that when the constitutional convention of South Carolina under the call of President Johnson met at

Columbia, although not myself a member of that convention, I urged on my friends who were members the necessity of opening at once the franchise to both races, without distinction, but making an educational and property qualification. But the sentiment of the South was not yet ripe for such a policy. If such qualifications could have been made at that time, the South would have been saved all the horrors of carpet-bag rule. But it is vain to indulge regret. I suppose it was impossible at that time, not only because the South was unprepared, but also because even if it had been done it would not have been accepted by Congress. Now, however, that the State governments are fully established, it can be done if the whites really desire it. Some qualification separating the capables from the incapables, the worthy from the unworthy, is probably the greatest want of the country everywhere. It can be done more easily at the South than anywhere else, because the necessity is greater, and because of the wider difference between the intelligent and unintelligent classes there.

Some feeble attempts have been made in this direction in certain parts of the South, and always with the best effects. In many States a law making payment of a small poll-tax of one or two dollars a condition of voting disfranchises a large majority of the ignorant blacks. It disfranchises some whites, too, but this is no objection. Other and less justifiable but legal means have been used to diminish the incapable vote, such as the eight-ballot-box law in South Carolina. Mississippi alone has gone still farther in this direction, and that because the necessity was greater there than in most States. In the recent constitution of that State there is a qualification for voting, including the ability to read, or else to understand and interpret the constitution and laws (a much harder condition than mere ability to read, but too indefinite), and also the payment of all taxes, including a poll-tax of two dollars, for the two preceding years. May we not hope that these qualifications will be increased in amount and extended throughout the South, and that they will become an entering wedge to accomplish the same result throughout the whole country?

It was thought by some that limitation of suffrage would diminish representation in Congress. This is still an open question, but probably it would not. (See Cooley, General Provisions of Constitutional Law, pp. 263, 264.) But, in any case, if the South is not willing to sacrifice something for the sake of good government, she does not deserve it.*

SOME PRINCIPLES OF THE ETHICAL PROBLEM DISCUSSED.

The classes of society, the principles on which they are based, and how far they are rational and just, this is the question which must now be discussed, for the so-called race-line is of this nature. The whites and blacks at the South are absolutely separated in society. They have separate churches, separate schools, separate colleges, and in large measure separate cars, separate hotels, etc. In the present state of feeling the Negroes themselves—many of them—prefer it so. Is the state of feeling right? It is evident that this question requires a discussion of some very fundamental ethical principles.

Nature is so complex that it can not be understood until simplified by classification. Things and phenomena can not be dealt with as individuals, for they are too numerous and diversified; they must be dealt with in groups or classes. The grouping of forces and phenomena constitutes physical science; the grouping of forms and objects, natural history. The process of grouping in physical science is called generalization, in natural history classification. This grouping is the most fundamental process in the construction of science. Either name would do, but we shall usually call it classification, because we will deal with grouping of forms and objects.

Now, man's mission on the earth is to understand Nature. But see the dilemma in which the human mind finds itself. It is impossible to advance a single step in science—i. e., in the rational comprehension of Nature—without classification; and yet a true classification—i. e., one that expresses the true relations of things—is impossible without complete scientific knowledge. Therefore he is compelled to make an arbitrary, artificial, provisional classification of some sort, to enable him to manage his material. Any classification is better than none; any kind of order is better than chaos. By the use of this provisional classification science or ra-

---

* Colonization has been proposed as an easy solution of the problem. Some of the most intelligent of the Negroes themselves—for example, Bishop Turner, of the African Methodist Church—earnestly advocate this plan. I say nothing of this plan, (1) because the Negroes very naturally refuse to colonize, (2) because the whites themselves would be loath to lose so valuable a laboring class, and (3) because this method would not touch the general question of race-contact.

3

tional knowledge is gradually accumulated, and this knowledge becomes, in its turn, the basis of a natural classification. But, unfortunately, often, especially in higher and more complex departments of thought, the provisional character of the first classification is not recognized, and the change into a more natural classification, which ought to take place gradually as science advances, is resisted by a too rigid conservatism, and, therefore, can only take place by revolution.

This law of the advance of rational thought is so fundamental and important that I must try to make it clear by illustrations. I might use for this purpose any department of science, but I select botany as the best.

The object of the botanist is to make a perfect natural classification of plants—i. e., a classification which shall express perfectly the natural affinities or degrees of kinship, or order of evolution of all plants. But, on the one hand, it is impossible to make such a classification without exhaustive knowledge of plants; on the other, it is impossible to begin to acquire such knowledge without a previous classification. How did the botanist emerge from this dilemma? He made first an artificial classification. Under the light and guidance of this, scientific knowledge became possible, and by the co-operation of an army of workers in every part of the world it was steadily accumulated. In proportion as knowledge of true relations of plants increased a natural classification based on these became possible and gradually displaced the artificial, though at first not without some resistance.

Observe now the difference between these two kinds of classifications. The one is the condition of rational knowledge, and the agent of its initiation, and the other is the compendious expression of rational knowledge, and the agent of its continuous advance. The one is of necessity perfect, rigid, made at once out of hand, as all artificial things are; the other is never perfect, but ever growing, evolving, as all natural things do, in order to adapt itself to an ever-growing knowledge, until finally it again disappears in the light of a perfect knowledge of individuals and their relations. Thus, when rational knowledge is perfect, like that of God, then classification or generalization will have done its perfect work and disappear. Or, to put it in another way: In artificial classification the division lines between classes are sharp, hard, and fast; in natural classification, and in proportion as it is natural, classes shade into each other more and more until the division lines disappear. Thus, the human mind starting from animal sense-perception of individuals without relations, passes through classification, and finally reaches perfect rational perception of individuals and their relations—from chaos through artificial order to rational order.

This law meets us in every department of thought and of human activity. It meets us, therefore, in the classification of society. The relations of individuals to one another are so numerous, diverse, and complex that they form at first a bewildering chaos. Now, man is put here in this world and the problem given him to solve is a rational classification or organization of society. But, on the one hand, such an organization is impossible without a complete knowledge of human relations—i. e., a complete sociology; on the other, such knowledge is impossible without a previous organization. Therefore, the first step in civilization is the classification of individuals on some obvious basis, however artificial and arbitrary, as the very condition of civilization and of rational knowledge. Any classification is better than none. It may be based on conquest, or on race, or on wealth, or on family, or on pursuit in life, or on any other obvious distinction. Then, with the advance of science or rational knowledge this classification must be modified and made more and more rational. In the ideal society, when sociology is complete and the moral nature of man perfect, when rational knowledge of human relations and the will to act in accordance with these relations is perfect, then I suppose classes of society, as we now know them, will have served their purpose and disappear. In other words, every man's position in the estimation of his fellow-men will be determined wholly by his real worth in every way, but especially his intellectual and moral worth. The non-recognition of this law is the cause of all revolutions.

Now, this law applies, of course, to the classes or castes of society as they exist to-day, and is their sufficient justification. In early stages of society these are arbitrary, artificial, rigid, separated by hard and fast lines impossible to overpass. In so far as they are so, they are unnatural and oppressive. But they were thoroughly recognized and regarded as inevitable, and society was therefore comparatively peaceful. They are now becoming less and less rigid, less and less impassable, especially in this country; but also their artificiality, their irrationality, and therefore injustice, are more and more recognized, and therefore society is becoming more and more restive. The time has come when classes of society must on the one hand be put on a more rational basis, and on the other must be recognized as a necessary condition of civilization.

Now, race-classes not only come under the same head, but are more natural and rational than many others, because founded on a real natural difference—i. e., a difference in the grade of evolution ; and, moreover, where the difference is as great as it is between the Anglo-Saxon and the Negro, the class-distinction seems absolutely necessary, at least for the present. This class-distinction, therefore, is peculiar, in that it is more rational than others in so far as it is more natural, but less rational in so far as the separating line (race-line) is more rigid and impassable, and partakes of the nature of caste. This natural caste-line can not be broken down, and, as it seems to me, ought not, until we understand better than we now do the laws of the effects of race-mixture. If the effects of the mixture of the extreme primary races be bad, not only immediately, but for all time and under any mode of regulation, then the law of organic evolution, the law of destruction of the lower races and the survival of only the higher, must prevail and the race-line must never be broken over. If, on the other hand, mixture of the extreme primary races can in any way and by any rational mode of regulation be made to elevate the human race, then the race-line must and ought to be broken down and complete mixture must eventually take place. We are not yet prepared to speak confidently on this subject.

Meanwhile, the exercise of mutual forbearance and kindness—in other words, of a true rational spirit—will do much even to mitigate or even to remove entirely the evils of the race-line. We must wait and let the problem solve itself. If only the spiritual brotherhood be realized, it will matter little if the physical distinction remain.

ABSTRACT OF THE DISCUSSION.

Mr. James A. Skilton:

I was extremely fortunate in having the privilege of opening the discussion of the paper read by Prof. Mason on the Land Problem, and am not less so in having the privilege of opening the discussion of the thoroughly scientific and very valuable paper read this evening by the distinguished president of the American Society for the Advancement of Science.

Prof. Le Conte has treated the subject not only from the scientific and evolutionary point of view, but also from the point of view of the sincere and thoughtful man of Southern birth and experience. It has been my fortune, however, to have approached the subject from the opposite point of view of Northern birth and experience, supplemented by an extended and unique experience in the same Southern State, in the "black belt," and practically in the locality of Prof. Le Conte's birth and early life, where before the war I took an organized force of white laborers and had the immediate control at different times of free white labor and slave labor, with abundant opportunity for instructive study and comparison. In so far as I was capable, I then, and have since, applied to the study of the subject scientific and evolutionary principles, and, as for my own candor and sincerity, it is sufficient to say that these may be considered as necessarily implied in the application of such principles.

It was my fortune to begin to study Southern conditions on the spot in December, 1852, and to approach the subject with caution, followed by years of deliberation, only to reach the broader conclusions I shall present to you under the illuminating processes and effects of growing secession and war and what has since developed from them. When every man of my white force was struck down with malarial fever and I was left alone and unaided to take care of my house, stock, and crops, I began to feel that my tuition in Southern conditions was commencing in earnest; and when forced to hire slaves to take their places or quit, I faced the situation, hired the slaves, and in due time got my practical experience on the slave-labor side as I had before done on the free-labor side, both in a Southern locality. Furthermore, with the slaves employed to take the places of white men disabled by malarial fevers, I not only came into direct contact as master by hire, but, being recognized by them as coming from the land of freedom, had to an unusual degree their confidence and trust in general, and frequently as to the deeper experiences of their personal and family lives.

It is usually very instructive, after having been put through a hard curriculum and learned your lesson, to watch others—those of different types, origins, and capacities—while they are being put through the same curriculum. This advantage I had in scores if not in hundreds of instances where the new scholars were Northern men or foreigners, newer or later comers in the South than myself, and thus have been able to review, reconsider, or verify my own observations and conclusions times without number.

Let me claim, then, that what I have to say is not presented as the view of a man of Northern birth who has recently begun the study of the subject, and, fresh from his first excursion, attempts to solve the Southern problem through the opportunities of a week's travel and of glimpses caught through the windows of a railroad car or of lessons learned in conversation with casual fellow-travelers. Having lived there and engaged in business, become a citizen, a voter, and subjected myself to all the influences of the Southern environment, I certainly have had the opportunity of obtaining an insight deeper than that of a transient person and of learning to understand and sympathize with the Southerner in the stupendous difficulties of his problem. In so doing I am glad to be able to say, nevertheless, that, scientific and evolutionary principles aiding me, I have never found myself compelled to sacrifice the broader Northern principles, properly so called, in which I was born and bred; certainly not my faith in freedom.

The truth of the matter is, the usual or current Northern and Southern views are neither of them sound or correct, and they never have been so. The real truth consists, and always has consisted, in a newer composite view that takes in parts of each, mainly the facts of the Southern view and the aspirations and hopes of the Northern view.

I have dwelt so much upon preliminaries because many years of experience have shown me the futility of the attempt to aid people to understand the real South unless they can be somehow, at least temporarily, dislocated from contemplation of the old view and so prepared to consider a different view.

To me, then, this opportunity is so unique that it can not well be repeated. I shall therefore spend no time on direct criticism of the paper of Prof. Le Conte in detail, but, hoping to equal him only in candor and sincerity, prefer to start from the opposite geographical point of the compass, and, in so far as the time permits, place my own thought parallel with his for the purposes of comparison as the method most likely to be instructive and beneficial; for then in those matters in which there is agreement there will be re-enforcement, and in those matters in which there is disagreement, if any, there will be opportunity for further study if necessary.

From my own point of view the race question may be treated—indeed, must be treated—as a continuation or extension of the land question.* Either actually or by implication the facts of the race question and race conditions being placed alongside of or correlated with those of land questions and conditions, which as the product of an almost purely selfish commercial policy have resulted in destroying opportunity for proper growth and development, the inference will be either drawn or held in mind that the very existence of a race question is due to the mismanagement or misdirection of economic forces, and that the solution of the question can only be found in a change of commercial policy dictated by rightly managed and directed economic principles and forces; and I shall further proceed on the larger generalization advanced by Dr. Lyman Abbott, in his letter read at the last meeting, to the effect that our race question is "simply the problem of man," and no mere negro question or Afro or Afric-American question.

But here let me dispose of one branch of the topic in a word. If the system of land barbarization, which beyond question has located the negro where he is and to some extent made him what we find him there, is to continue, then for me the race question is already settled— I do not wish to see the white man enter a contest the goal of which is permanent barbarism. By all means let the most barbarous or the least civilized race capture and possess that goal without contest on the part of the race to which I belong, if natural or climatic law, the laws of commerce or society, present no alternative.

The really difficult parts of the race problem are chiefly due to hallucinations or misinformations. When these are disposed of it may be a matter of doubt whether any race problem remains. When we get below them and among the real **facts of** the case, we find **that the negro is** as much the product of evolution as any other race, **that he** belongs by nature and by history to the hotter and necessarily **more** backward regions of the world, to and in which he is constitutionally suited and the white race totally unsuited. Indeed, these facts show that while the blacks may not have the qualities required to civilize the temperate zones, the whites have shown no capacity for civilizing the tropics, and that the two races are therefore quits. Seemingly, we would prefer to take the negro out of his natural domain, in violation of evolutionary law and result, and force him to adapt himself to a new habitat instead of building on what has been done by Nature in the

* See The Land Problem, pp. 111 and 131.

past and helping to civilize his habitat and thereby the man and the race. If the white race would first really develop the fit civilization of its own habitat by following the true lines of sociological growth, it would then be in a position to assist the negro to do the same thing where he belongs, each thus aiding and neither hindering the other. Looking at the matter in this way, we may see that our duty is to build on the negro as he is rather than to attempt to reconstruct him on the plan of the white man. It is certain that the negro is in the world for a purpose, with a fitness at least to accomplish beneficent ends, if we can manage to understand, respect and aid in the application of the necessary means to accomplish those ends. And when we look him over and over and through and through, glancing our eyes between times at the conditions and possibilities of the hotter regions of the world to which he belongs, we will, if sufficiently clear-sighted, begin to suspect that about the worst use we could put him to would be to make him over on the white man's pattern ; unless it be the substitution of a mongrel race in the place of the two races.

There is one almost universal hallucination lying here at the threshold and requiring removal before we can even properly enter upon discussion. In the first place, slavery was essentially a condition. It never was essentially an institution. It has been our great mistake that we have treated it as such, and only as such. It was a growth— in fact, an evolutionary growth. And as a condition it never was destroyed, never can be destroyed, either by a proclamation of emancipation, by a mere constitutional amendment, or by any other mere institutional means or method. Without going into an explanation of these statements, it is sufficient to quote the words of the master:

" No one can be perfectly free till all are free ; no one can be perfectly moral till all are moral ; no one can be perfectly happy till all are happy."

In other words, freedom, morality, and happiness must be universal or they can not exist. They must be the product of a universal condition—a condition in which the unity is created out of diversity by growth, by evolution.

While the ex-slaves of the South have since emancipation, so called, come into a time when they can claim political freedom and point to the fundamental law in support of that claim, they still remain under the dominion of the same economic and industrial law and condition in and by which they were originally made slaves, and can never become in fact free men—without something more than mere institutional change. Having no genuine economic freedom, they can have no real political or social freedom.

There is another point that needs clearing up to the Northern mind. Under slavery the slave was in essential particulars the pet of the system. His white master, the master's wife, and their children looked after him with the most earnest and incessant care; not only did the lady of the plantation personally attend and nurse him when sick, but when he was assaulted the slave had his master for a protector; and I have myself seen an avenging master pursuing the white murderer of his slave, pistol in hand, with the same terrible expression on his face that he might have had if his son instead of his slave had been the victim of attack. In slavery, therefore, the position of the slave was in essential respects ostensibly better than that of the poor white who lived on his little clearing near by, and had no protector or avenger but himself. For the slave was assisted by his master in his struggle for survival and elevation in the scale of life. So far as this is concerned, therefore, emancipation threw the slave back on to the same level with the poor white, leaving him only the aid of the past benefits and protection of slavery to give him help in the battle of the future, certain to be of doubtful value.

And, fruitful as this age has been in opera bouffe, it is doubtful if any production in that line equals the performance of the abolitionists when, immediately after the war, they assembled in solemn council, disbanded their abolition societies, delivered their orations of self-praise, and marched off from the battle-field with drums beating and banners flaunting the air, at the very moment when the results of the war furnished them the opportunity to begin the battle for freedom as a condition in the South. No history of the past and no working scheme for the elevation of the negro in the future can miss or ignore the deep significance of this point and be of any value whatever. Practically the abolitionists treated freedom as well as slavery as institutional in character and origin; they understood neither the ultimate cause nor the cure of slavery, but left the matter of its abolishment in such confusion that we may credit them with the creation of the problem we are discussing, and for which no clear solution of their suggestion yet appears after more than a quarter of a century of further study and experience. In fact, the negro was practically abandoned by his so-called friends and left to the tender mercies of his so-called enemies and former masters; and, notwithstanding the masters had insisted that they could frame no theory or system according to which the industries of the South could be conducted on the basis of freedom, both the abolitionists and others at the North abandoned the negro, substantially, to his own devices, after giving him the franchise as the sole and sufficient panacea for all his ills past and to come.

The point I make is that, like the slave-holders, the abolitionists had no practical and just solution to offer, and that they ran away and turned the problem over to others, while claiming credit for a solution that was no solution. Not only was there no recognition by abolitionists then that slavery was the product of economic action, but, as many notable examples show, the economic policy* frequently, if not generally, advocated by them before and since the war was exactly that which took away " opportunity," and thereby produced slave conditions in the one case and actually prevented the development of free conditions in the other.

The dominant Southern idea before, during, and for a time after the war was that under emancipation and freedom the negro would certainly perish. Historical facts and evolutionary principles coincide with the proposition that the laborer is the member of society in and through whom that society survives, and that the so-called aristocrat is the man who perishes. If, therefore, the solution of the race problem in the South is the answer to the question, who will survive and eventually rule the region now occupied by the negro, mainly in the black belt, as a mere race contest in the midst of unchanged economic status and action ? The only thing left to be said is that the negro will unquestionably survive and possess the land, and the relative status of the two races in that region will eventually be changed in his favor. That is to say, if the industrial and economic conditions that have caused his numerical predominance in that region are to continue, he as their fit product will certainly survive and win ; and with him an ethical, intellectual, and social standard of a co-ordinate character, tempered by the limited and inadequate eleemosynary aid of his Northern friends, will also win. For, as these friends are only now beginning to discover, they have labor problems at home at the

---

* I mean the free-trade policy, and have particularly in mind my friend and pastor Henry Ward Beecher and his immediate followers. Even now that he is dead, I believe that, unless his influence in this direction can be checked and counteracted, far greater injury will come (not only to the ex-slave, so called, but to mankind) than of service from his life and work, great as that service seems to me to have been. I do not undertake to decide the question, but only to raise it for consideration, and this in the interest of his future fame as the ages come and go.

The history of the nomenclature of abolition, itself and alone, sustains, if it does not establish, my view. Primarily and derivatively *abolition* is abolescence, or *growth from* the thing abolished. *Webster* so derives and defines the word. But *The Century Dictionary* distinctly shows the influence and effect of abolitionist philosophy and action during the past fifty years, in the all but complete elimination of the idea of growth from the current definition of the word, and the substitution of ideas purely mechanical and artificial in its place.

The favorite word *emancipation*, defining the abolitionist achievement, completes the demonstration. Whether the release be from the hand of purchase or from that of capture, the expression is entirely and carefully mechanical, and it follows the hard, unyielding Roman law out of which the stiff, wooden system of our present social structure has been largely built, and into which it is one of our objects to somehow breathe the breath of something like life and growth. Abolitionism has, therefore, not only failed to apply the necessary evolutionary principles of growth to the solution of the slavery and race problems, but, in addition to debasing our political methods to the level of the inorganic, has done the same thing for the English language and the nomenclature of the subject, and even for its very name. In other words, abolitionism has betrayed the fundamental principle of its propaganda as expressed in the title it so proudly wears. And as to method, it set the bad example which other reforms are now fatally following because of its supposed success.

North to solve, for which no solution yet appears, that must tax Northern resources to the verge of failure at least. That region will then become substantially only a possibly better Africa, with which American statesmanship must deal on that comparatively low level; for the Southern poor white, although always free politically, has not been able to rise above **and out of the characteristic Southern** status. Nor will the man **of the inferior race be able to do so, as we** must conclude when we **consider the lesser opportunities he has had here and elsewhere for ages past.**

The significant fact mentioned by Prof. Le Conte as to the want of return to him, ever since emancipation, from lands that had supported his ancestors and their slaves for generations, shows at least a tendency toward the disappearance of the white man and his civilization from the black belt first of **all.**

But does that portion of the United States ultimately belong to the negro through ethnological, climatic, economic, and industrial, or, in other words, through ultimate evolutionary title deeds? That territory was not his original habitat; he was dragged into it by the force of barbarous economic principles and practice. In climate and in almost every other respect it is unlike any other habitat in which unmodified evolutionary law and development have located him. His African home lies between the isothermal lines of 68° F. The black belt lies entirely above and outside of that line and in the climatic home of the white race. That region belongs climatically either to the white man or to one of the other races; primarily to the red race, whose problem is being rapidly decided by extinction, somewhat on the theory of General Sherman—that the only good Indian is a dead Indian. And in so far as the red man had prior title, the white man is his natural **heir** and successor, and not the black man, notwithstanding the white man, like the black man, belongs to an imported race. **As to** the future and the right **of** the negro to continue in dominant occupancy of the South, or any part of it, as before intimated, it depends, **I** may say, entirely on the highest ideal status of civilization possible of achievement in that region.

As for myself, that question was experimented with and decided on the spot in favor of the white man more than thirty years ago, and the development of evolutionary science and philosophy within that time has furnished a succession of confirmations of the conclusion. After myself working in the field with white men, and also with slaves, I am prepared to say that the only seemingly natural and important obstruction or hindrance to the occupation of that country and to the performance **of the** necessary labor everywhere for its development by the white man, **is,** not high temperature, but the presence in many localities of malaria, to which the white man is only less resistant * than the black man. And it is both a scientific and a historical fact that the malaria is the direct product of a barbarous economic system which produces the land barbarization, and slavery, of which it is a symptom. It has not always been dominant there in the past, and therefore may not continue to be dominant in the future, under a different system. It has increased co-ordinately with slavery.

Does it seem possible or probable that a region of country located so near elevated regions manifestly the natural home of the white man, and the white man of civilization, can belong scientifically and naturally, in this age, to the black man, as its dominant occupier and exploiter?

What then is to be said about the physical degeneracy of Confederate soldiers of those regions who outmarched and outfought Union soldiers so frequently during the war?

What about the lecturer of the evening, president of the leading scientific association of America, a leader in evolutionary study and thought, indeed, in important departments the leader, in America, and known to be such throughout Europe; and, besides, a long list of distinguished names of several generations in the same family? This, too, not an isolated, exceptional instance. Liberty County, Georgia, where he was born and bred, was, many generations since, settled by people from New England, who started from good old Dorchester, Mass., as did the first settlers of Windsor and Hartford, Conn., re-enforced by a strong contingent of Huguenot blood. I venture to say that no purely agricultural county in the United States has produced a greater number of distinguished men than that county. Early in the fifties I became acquainted with a number of its inhabitants, saw many more, and learned their history. Liberty County touches salt water between the Savannah and Altamaha Rivers. It is marked on the map as black as the blackest in the black belt, its oldest town Dorchester. As I saw and knew them, they were large, finely built, red-cheeked, masterful men—more like the original type of New England settler than any other men I ever saw, even in New England.

Of course the uneducated mind accepts what is as what must be; but the mind imbued with evolutionary ideas recognizes it as a fundamental principle that what now is can not continue to be; for, unless progress is made, decline is inevitable. The causes which have barbarized land and the people living on it continuing, through increased soil exhaustion, deeper barbarism is certain to be reached.

---

* The negro's power of resisting malaria seems to have declined in his new home in the South. I found the chief difference between the two races in the matter of resisting malarial poisons to be that whereas the white man could neither work nor eat, the negro could eat but not work. And in this fact, also, we may find a hint as to survival and eventual lapse into savagery and wilderness if the conditions continue.

There was a time in the early history of the black belt—in its eastern part—before land barbarization had done its work and the slave system had been developed, when malaria did not prevail, and it is only a question of a possible civilized and civilizing method of treating the soil as the result of which malaria may be eliminated. When that method is adopted, the atmospheric temperature of the country will be found not unsuitable or deleterious to the white laborer, and the superior value of the Southern products will give the white man a much greater return for the same labor, as compared with the grain-producing regions of the North. When to the opportunities of the field are added those of the factory, and the manufacture of cotton in or near the place of its production, an enormous increase of white population will certainly take place; and rich as the region is in deposits of phosphates and other marine products, capable as it is of producing enormous crops of vegetable food suitable only for consumption near its place of production, and fit to give the white man physical strength and intellectual force, it certainly may be expected that, even with no removal of the negro as a race, the country will become possessed by the white man in such force and numbers as to place the negro in the same relative position that he occupies at the North. This will keep the political and social power of those regions in the hands of the race occupying the Eastern, Middle, Western, and Pacific States—one and homogeneous, and settle the race question in the South as it has done elsewhere.

Under the exigencies of the war, mechanics were in great demand in the South, and the "black belt," even, became dotted with developing manufacturing enterprises which continued to flourish down to Appomattox day, and under a proper system there is no reason why they should not be revived and become permanent.

It will be impossible on this occasion to even catalogue the forces and principles that will support that movement in civilizing this region when once the corner is turned. The story of the Garden of Eden does not furnish the principal evidence that through degradation man and vegetation suffer together, while thorns and thistles flourish. Science teaches the same lesson. The history of the South confirms it. The barbarization of the land and its people is found to be both coincident and co-ordinate with the deterioration of the fiber of the cotton in length, quality, and value, as the strength of the soil diminishes. When the system is changed and soil enrichment takes the place of soil impoverishment, exactly the opposite will occur, the staple will be increased in length of fiber, improved in quality and quantity, other kinds of plant life will also thrive and improve, and, step by step, the problems of man, society, and the state will be co-

ordinately and coincidently advanced and solved. No such development, however, can occur except with and through an entire abandon-
ment of the old system and an increase of common interest and commercial relations between the farms and shops of the North and the
farms and shops of the South, and also between the cities of the North
and the cities of the South; in fact, between the two hitherto diverse
and antagonistic civilizations. The result of this diversity—which
includes diversity of interests—has been war in the past and will inevitably be war in the future, in one form or another, unless a law of
harmony is discovered and put in practice. A result of proper increased commercial exchange between the North and the South would
be a tendency to check soil exhaustion, effect soil enrichment in both
regions, and bring about unity of interests. But a most important
and further effect of a dominant white civilization, not only in the
upland region of the South but also in the cotton and lowland region,
must be the development of increased commercial interchange between
the people of these regions and the adjacent peoples of the West
Indian, Mexican, Central American, and South American regions, the
more accessible and near-by portions, of course, having the advantage,
other things being equal. One of our statesmen said, during the San
Domingo debate, that republics should "beware of the tropics," referring evidently to the effects of the overmastering power of vegetal
growth in preventing or checking the development of man and society.
Evolutionary economics clearly points to the gradual movement toward equilibration of agricultural wealth between the lands of the
tropic and the temperate zones as the means of benefiting the peoples
of both, and therefore to the true basis for a scientific commercial
system not only for America but for the world. Such commercial relations will inevitably be beneficial to the West Indies, and must lead
to the ending of European domination therein, to more and more
affiliation with the people of the United States, and eventually to the
furnishing of a market and opportunity for the free black labor of the
South to emigrate to the West India Islands, there to find increased
reward and a more natural climate, through the increased demand in
the near-by South for all sorts and kinds of tropical productions, and
a counter-demand in those islands for the productions of all parts of
the United States. Under this condition of things there would be a
tendency and movement of agricultural products, and the means they
furnish for the enrichment of the soil, from the tropical regions of the
farther south to the Southern portion of the United States first, and
eventually to the Northern portion of the United States.

The history of Florida and its renewed relations with the North
and its people since 1865 is an instructive study in this connection.

In 1835 these relations were cut or destroyed by the ruin of the orange groves in that year, the effects of which lasted for thirty years. As the increased crop of Florida fruit has found an increasing market at the North since 1865-'66, Northern people have more and more found occupation and homes in Florida, largely neglecting the intermediate regions that furnish no such products. The same principle will apply on the larger scale, including the West India Islands, in the development of dominant commercial movements on north and south lines substantially at right angles to those of dominant commercial movement under the present system.

This would develop a commerce based on soil enrichment and higher civilization everywhere in the United States, as against a system of commercial interchange based on soil exhaustion and consequent barbarization, as now, under what I may call the English system, although it has become the system of the world. So far as this country is concerned, at least, that system insists and must insist on commercial movements on east and west lines, whereby, through the continually cheapening cost of transportation, our agricultural products are removed forever from the country and exchanged for Brummagim and other wares, which, however they may be disposed of, and whatever may be their value otherwise, certainly can not do much in the way of refertilizing our wheat and grain fields or the cotton fields of the South. Necessary result, the destructive competition of like with like.

Our fathers started out to establish an American continental system in and under which the rights of all men should be respected. Their children have been in the main content to undertake and continue to manage a continent on parochial principles, and these inextricably and intentionally confused by constant and universal European interference. This sufficiently explains the failures of the past and the hopes and possibilities of the future.

There are two ways of stating my position :

1. There is no race question except as we make one through our failure to recognize and apply the scientific principles of an advancing civilization in their land and ethnological relations and implications, working harmoniously to the desired end.

2. The solution of the race question is to be found by giving to each race its own fit habitat and the opportunities belonging to each, in which each race will help others without antagonisms, either political or social, each furnishing a market for the products of the other.

Under a system of this kind, so rich in possibilities is the black-belt region that it could support a population as large as the present population of the United States, of which only a small and unobtrusive fraction would be black, while the West Indies and Central America would fill up with a black race partly composed of emigrants from the United States constantly growing in civilization through the necessary effects of "opportunity" furnished by a near-by market. It would matter little whether the two races worked under the same flag or not, so long as they worked in peace and prospered through the results of a common interest in a commerce scientifically based on the different natural productions of different soils, climates, and regions. Only a continental system could accomplish such results. A continental system is impossible so long as any part of the continent or of the adjacent islands is occupied and held under European dominion and governed by European ideas, North or South; and here we reach the root of the whole matter. It is not plain piracy and plunder now as formerly, but the European idea is that America must be held in a commercial sense tributary to Europe for the purpose of aiding European governments in governing European peoples on European plans and principles, whatever may become of American governments, peoples, and plans. We have accepted that relation not only as to commerce in goods, but also in the commerce of ideas, which they supply in support of their plans and principles and which we accept and adopt although they attack and overthrow American plans and principles. Not so was it with the fathers. They saw the need if not the opportunity of setting up an independent continental system and elected a Continental Congress to begin with. When their descendants have wisdom enough and force enough to complete the plans of the fathers in a continental system with which Europe is not allowed to injuriously interfere, then we shall find solutions not only for race problems, but for many other problems that are now not much less vexing and obscure. When that day comes there will be no fine questions to discuss as to the effects of the mixing of races and race contacts, because there will be a common and universal interest in keeping the races pure and unmixed until at least an equal culture, wealth, and social status shall remove the natural and beneficent race prejudice—if they ever do. Independent race improvement for each in its own natural habitat may then proceed in an orderly and peaceful manner, the combative instincts of men being directed to the subduing or at least training and using the forces of Nature as the true policy of progress. Freedom from European commercial and economic interference is the most important factor in the solution of this as of many other problems.

If Europe and European methods and ideas could be persuaded or forced to let go their deadly grip on the people of all outlying countries of the world, it is by no means impossible that something more than a destiny of destruction might be found for the so-called lower races of other types without intermixture of blood or absorption even.

Necessarily, in the presence of such a solution the political and associated moral difficulties of the problem would largely disappear.

Here, as throughout, the key to the situation is justice. Justice between men, and justice—or obedience to the law of right—toward land in its broadest interpretation, failing which the land has its own slow but sure system of punishment for wrong-doers.

But injustice to land and to the negro is not the only injustice that has had to do with the creation of this question. There is, in fact, another question of race or part of a race still more obscure than the negro race question, upon which the solution of the latter absolutely depends. In spite of slavery and the conditions in which it flourished, a distinct type of men had been developed there which naturally affiliated with the peoples of the North to a marked degree in their ideas and aspirations about freedom, union, and related topics. These men doubted the beneficence of slavery and would have been glad to join the North in some reasonable plan for getting rid of it. Singularly enough, no discussions note or explain the total absence of this one important factor in the solution. In nearly all the seceding States Union men were in the majority in 1860. These Union men were not only the natural allies and friends of the Union before the war, but they were also the natural leaders of reconstruction and the natural friends, teachers, and leaders of the negro in his induction into political opportunity and the new status. They seem to have disappeared from the face of the earth as effectually as the ten tribes of Israel, all in one generation, leaving no sign. What happened to them and what has become of them? Having clearly seen the opportunity they were possibly to have after the war, as early as the fall of 1860, having been one of them myself, having been an observant witness of the deep damnation of their taking off, and having done my best to prevent it at the time, there is a certain duty of explanation laid upon me.

In some minds before the election, and in many within forty-eight hours after it, the great and urgent questions were: If we have separation in peace, what will be the status and fate of Union men? If secession is followed by war, what? Between the upper and nether mill-stones of the contention, how are we and our rights to fare? And when it is all over, who is to rule in these Southern States and who is to be ruined, the Secessionist or the Unionist, especially if the Union conquers? Will not the Government ignore us, make terms with their enemies and ours after the war, and put us under their heels forever? These were the supreme questions to the Southern Unionist.

It was at once seen by myself and many others that England, repre-

4

senting herself and foreign interests in general, would probably exercise as much influence in settling our fate and that of the negro as either the Confederacy or the United States, perhaps more—and more it turned out to be.

International law and the laws of war have been established by governments of the imperial order and conform to their interests and principles; and against them we seem to have no courage to protest. In that system whatever the king does every one of his subjects constructively does and may be held responsible for accordingly by the king of the nation with which their king may be at war. But American citizens never were subjects of any king. They were and are sovereigns, each in his own right. How, then, could any man or combination of men, minority or majority, by setting up a State or Confederate government in rebellion and committing treason for themselves, also commit treason and work forfeiture of rights of any kind—property, life, franchise, representation, protection of every kind—for any other citizen and sovereign, and especially for a Union citizen who opposed them with all the powers the Government placed in his hands, and more besides, when even the Government itself was powerless to prevent rebellion and treason by any means at its command?

Starting from this foundation during the winter of 1860-'61, I personally originated and worked out a plan for the protection of the Southern Unionist and to enable him to aid the United States in putting down rebellion, preserving the State autonomy in himself and his class, taking in hand the management of the States in reconstruction, and generally showing the South how to enter upon the new civilization of freedom, peace, and Union after the war. It included a plan to enable the Government to separate the sheep from the goats when the day of victory and judgment should come.

My plan rested upon the claim that, unless forfeited by some act of the individual, the right of representation in Congress remained to the Union man of the South; that no rights of the Unionist could be forfeited by residence within the States in which rebellious citizens had attempted to establish a new State government or a new general government, not even when *de facto* successful in that attempt; and that the property of Union men was protected by the Constitution and could not be confiscated for constructive treason even when running the blockade outward, especially if done in obedience to a proclamation of the President calling upon Southern citizens to withdraw themselves and refrain from aiding and abetting treason and rebellion. Two months or more were spent in Washington during June, July, and August, 1861, in pressing these and related points upon the attention of the executive, legislative, and judicial departments of the Government. Among those personally approached were Mr. Lincoln, Thad. Stevens, Judge Wayne, Senator Ira Harris, of New York, and Mr. Dawes, of Massachusetts, the latter occupying the controlling position of chairman of the Committee on Elections of the House. The first four were prompt to see the importance of the suggestions made, and Mr. Stevens, then chairman of the Committee of Ways and Means, embodied the suggestion to put a tax on cotton, intended to act practically like an export duty, which was subsequently declared unconstitutional after some seventy-five millions had been collected, which still remain in the United States Treasury. Mr. Dawes (looking at the matter with the eyes of parochial statesmanship) saw a deep-laid plot of treason in giving Southern Unionists their right of representation even for the purpose of keeping the South divided into two parties, one for and the other against the Government, and used his influence on the floor of the House and elsewhere to prevent it.

Others besides myself were urging the same policy for similar reasons; but Union representation from seceded States was denied and the Union elements were abandoned to their fate, many of them to be forced to co-operate with the secession elements, however unwillingly, thereby practically uniting the South in the compact body which resisted so long and cost so much to conquer.

The fatal influence that produced this result was that of the English Government, with its watchful eyes on the blockade and Southern trade and its policy of embarrassment in order to make the rebellion successful. It became evident that if Southern Unionists were represented in Congress, British ships would insist on entering Southern ports in order to trade with the Southern people, on the theory that under a *de facto* government all or none were in rebellion. That is to say, the commercial system which resulted in slavery and rebellion through soil exhaustion had established relations that made or seemed to make it the interest of England to destroy the Union and the Union people of the South. The same relations still continue and furnish one of the great obstacles to the solution of our race and other problems.

The consequence was that, in spite of the fundamental principles of justice and without voluntary acts of treason on which to justify the treatment, the United States in all its departments—executive, judicial, and legislative—treated its friends, the Union men in the South, as just as guilty as its enemies, emancipating their slaves without compensation, confiscating their property as that of public enemies, taking away their right of representation, and finally, without making the slightest distinction between friends and foes, tendering to those who had never committed treason an amnesty oath, in which without charge, trial, jury, or benefit of clergy even, they were made to confess treason and surrender all political rights and all property rights over twenty thousand dollars in value, as the sole condition and only means whereby they could take their letters from the post-office, do any business whatever, or continue to live in the South; and this amnesty oath was to be and was filed in the State Department at Washington, there to be held as proof in all coming time of crime against the Government, whether any such crime had ever been committed by the individual signing it or not. Even discharged soldiers and officers of the Union army who helped to put down the rebellion and had the proof of wounds on their bodies and of their discharges in their pockets were compelled to take the same oath. Indeed, it is quite possible, I believe certain, that the Government is now paying pensions to men whose amnesty oaths confessing treason are at this moment on file in the State Department. Such are the travesties of governmental administration and justice.

This was the treatment, in outline, that destroyed Unionism in the South and deprived the emancipated slave of his natural and native friend, and also the Government itself.

I was one of ten persons summoned, by suggestion from Washington, to meet for the purpose of organizing the Republican party in the State of Georgia under the provisional Governor appointed by President Johnson—with a view to the election of the first State officers and a legislature. We had one meeting and adjourned *sine die.* There was no other course to pursue. No Republican party was then organized. The secession element, after slight surprise and hesitation and finally amusement over the preposterous folly of the Government policy, took the amnesty oath, elected their sort to office, and started in at once to nullify the results of the war. Why not ?

At this point Congress stepped in, gave the negro political rights, the secession elements retired, the Union elements existed no longer —had been destroyed by the Government's own acts—and the only element left was the famous carpet-bag contingent, the fit survival of the fittest out of all this combined burlesque and travesty of statesmanship.

Under such auspices as these did the solution of the race and other Southern problems commence. Should we wonder at the results we have seen and now see ? The United States Government, that for which the North was and is responsible, destroyed first the Union, and then the Disunion party of the South, leaving the field to transients. The carpet-bagger, who practically did all the work of restoration, has been blamed for all the blunders and crimes of the period, and his fate at the hands of the historians we may anticipate. But in fact he is only a convenient and somewhat amusing scarecrow in the Southern corn-field, rigged out in the tattered and torn mistakes and misfits of both sides to the original controversy. Neither side knowing what to do with the negro, then as now, and not offering to do anything, pretty much all the fault has been heaped upon him for doing something, all that was done, the best he knew of what to do. His answer to all the charges is most complete and sufficient. Like other scarecrows, of other corn-fields, he has been found capable of enduring all the storms and peltings that have fallen upon him, in silence, without giving any sign of any attempt at self-defense. This tactics on his part is sure to tire out his enemies eventually; and then will come their season for self-investigation, and the investigation of the race problem on its own separate and independent merits. Not forever will the real culprits, North and South, be able to unload their own faults and crimes upon the back of the wretched carpet-bagger.*

The significant fact remains as a perpetual lesson, that whereas before the war the whites were divided into two political parties, one of them favoring the Union and frequently in the majority, there is now, as the result of the insane injustice of the Government itself, practically but one party, which no "force bill" and no standing army can ever divide, because neither of them can touch the cause of that unity, but must instead substitute aggravation for remedy. A necessary preliminary to the solution of the negro race question in the South is the resurrection of the Union type of men in something like the old proportions by the sustained development of an economic policy that will permit such men to live and prosper there. That policy is the necessary policy of a higher civilization which has in it the energy to meet and overcome the policy of barbarization in the struggle for survival.

There is but one remedy—the establishment of the conditions of freedom and race co-operative unity. To establish these the United States must take the control of the interests of its own people at the

---

* But the carpet-bagger robbed the South, they say. Well, I am afraid he did. Doubtless when he saw shipwreck ahead he grabbed what he could lay hands on and got ashore, or North, the best way he could. But I venture to say, in all seriousness, and out of abundant opportunity of knowledge, that for every dollar he stole from the South, the South stole ten from him at least. Prof. Le Conte mentions the quick recuperation of the South after the war, notwithstanding the disorganization of labor. Largely the money of the carpet-bagger did it. Money was then abundant. Crowds of men went South to invest it and help rebuild on the new foundations. The chances are that ninety-nine out of every hundred dollars of that money was permanently invested there, and that the remaining dollar better represents what the carpet-bagger managed to get away with. Public clamor, and especially political public clamor, always makes such "ducks and drakes" of truth and fact. As for myself, I saw the thing coming and carpet-bagged out of the South before the negro *régime* began, impelled by unspeakable sorrow and disgust over the impending fiasco. But I know the history of hundreds of others, and I know of none who brought away more than a small fraction of what they took there. I further know of very many who never got away with their lives even, much less with their money.

bottom by breaking the hold of English commercial policy upon those interests, through some system of protection for the South against soil exhaustion and the removal of the "opportunities" of freedom, and this on some comprehensive continental plan, either of war or peace, or both, that shall eliminate English political, military, and commercial dominion from this continent and from all the adjacent islands.

It has been said by economists that if all the personal property of a civilized community should be destroyed, about three years' labor would furnish the means of restoration. The destruction of property in slaves by emancipation was not as disastrous as expected, in part because labor thereby became free to move, and did in part move, to more productive lands, thereby speeding recuperation, only to repeat the same old round of land destruction, however. But, under a system permitting soil enrichment from year to year, the capital in buildings, fences, and other improvements would be saved, and also that required to pay for new improvements on new lands, while the accompanying improved agriculture would require and develop superior intelligence and growing morality in the labor employed. This is the true line of march out of slavery into freedom, as also into freedom from race antagonisms.

Precisely here are to be found the origin and remedy of the unexpected race problems with which the North is beginning to be afflicted. A policy of soil exhaustion under the control of unchecked transportation interests and action on behalf of the owners and manipulators of railroads must create a demand for and assist the supply of an ever-deteriorating class of laborers, constantly lowering the standard of American citizenship everywhere. An opposite policy would have an opposite effect upon that standard, and would have a further effect to check the current tendency to railroad wrecking, trusteeships, reorganization, and general decline in value. It would also check the spirit of railroad conflict, competition, and homicide. Relief of race problems by education and improved morality depends upon increased return for labor, better wages. Cause and effect are found on both sides of the equation, but still the destruction of the poor is everywhere their poverty. The wages of workers are to society what food is to the body—they enrich, strengthen, and make healthy the life-blood of the social organism.

In these propositions will be found the answer to the question of Prof. Le Conte: "What is the best next step?" And all the answers may be summed up in a universal policy of land protection—protection against land destruction by the insidious effects of both foreign and domestic policies that rob the American worker of the material things on and by which alone his work can be employed, expended, and made fruitful. To accomplish this the continent must be surveyed, and out of its diversities a consistent continental policy of unity and harmony framed, adopted, put in practice, guarded against foreign and domestic interference; these steps to be repeated as often as enlightened progress may demand and permit.

The history of the rebellion, its antecedents and sequences, is so full of studies and instruction for the evolutionary sociologist, and this opportunity is so unique and little likely to be repeated, that one who was a witness with eyes wide open is loath to drop the subject. Let me refer briefly to one or two more points.

I have said elsewhere, substantially: Secession never won in the South until it appeared at last that the new autonomy would furnish opportunity to the young men of the South in the army and navy of the Confederacy. The new autonomy was the result of what naturalists know as propagation by fission, which takes place when the organism can no longer supply itself with the necessary amount of food. It might be called propagation by starvation or by poverty, and its application here would be more apparent by the use of either of these terms.

Now, portions of the Northern States are at this moment unconsciously getting ready for splitting up, propagating by fission, for the same reasons. New England, having exhausted its soil and other natural resources, is beginning to demand free trade, in order to obtain cheap Nova Scotia coal and hold her manufacturing enterprises. Meantime Quebec has largely annexed New England by sending over four hundred thousand French Canadians there, who propose to appropriate and control the whole of it through the effects of another form of propagation—the natural one—raised to the highest power under skillful priestly direction. Here we have the almost complete conditions for the formation of a new confederacy or dominion, including Quebec, New England, and that portion of the Dominion lying east of the St. Lawrence. Meanwhile our Protestant priesthood are squabbling over creeds and higher criticism, sacrificing birthright for pottage again.

Further, the combination of Union States was always wasp-waisted at or about the region of Ohio. But for the strong breed of New Englanders who first settled the northern part of that State, and the necessities of east and west commercial movement, a point for another fission might have been found there long since. When this east and west movement begins to decline, as it must before long, if it has not done so already, another danger spot, with or without a danger signal, will be found in Ohio. Further study would show other danger spots, if opportunity permitted.

What our fathers called Providence, and we may call evolution-

ary protection, or provision by compulsion—the necessity of raising
revenue by taxing the foreigner through an export duty—put into the
Confederate constitution the means for destroying slavery by slow
evolutionary action, and for building up a strong and prosperous people. This means the success of Union arms destroyed. It is for us to
take a lesson out of the same book. When we have done so, and en-
larged the teaching to cover a continental system, we may flatter our-
selves that we have begun to solve our race problems, and many other
equally important problems; and not till then.

Dr. Lewis G. Janes:

I wish to correct what I think might be a false impression from
the criticism of Mr. Skilton on the action of the abolitionists in dis-
banding their organization after the war. As I was brought up after
the strictest sect of the abolitionists, and read the discussions in their
papers when this action was taken, I think I can speak with authority
concerning their motives. They did not consider that their work was
done—that they had no further obligation to help the colored people,
as Mr. Skilton assumes. But they found themselves then in substan-
tial agreement with a large section—more than half—of their fellow-
countrymen. It seemed to them that they could exercise a wider
influence, and do better and more effective work for the colored man,
by breaking down the barrier of their exclusive organization and
joining hands with all those who were working for the same ends.
Whether they were right or not I will not argue; but I believe the
truth of history will recognize the purity of their motives, and their
life-long devotion, as individuals and citizens, to the welfare of the
colored race. I know personally that many of them had a wiser fore-
sight of the difficulties succeeding emancipation than most of their
Northern fellow-citizens. Many of them have since devoted years of
faithful service to the education and improvement of the freedmen.
Without arguing the question, I must also dissent from his policy of
expatriating the colored people, which it clearly seems to me would
result, not in their civilization, but in their relapse into utter barbarism, as in San Domingo.

Prof. Le Conte, in closing: At this late hour I will not detain
the audience by further remarks. I desire merely to extend my thanks
to the audience for their courteous attention, and especially to express
my great interest and general agreement with the remarks of Mr.
Skilton. It appears to me, speaking off-hand and under the impulse of
my present feeling, that he has indicated very nearly the true solution
of this problem.

D. APPLETON & CO.'S PUBLICATIONS.

MODERN SCIENCE SERIES.

Edited by Sir JOHN LUBBOCK, Bart., F. R. S.

The works to be comprised in the "Modern Science Series" are primarily **not for** the student, nor for the young, but for the educated layman who needs to know **the** present state and result of scientific investigation, and who has neither time nor inclination to become a specialist on the subject which arouses his interest. Each book will be complete in itself, and, while thoroughly scientific in treatment, its subject will, as far as possible, be presented in language divested of needless technicalities. Illustrations will be given wherever needed by the text. The following are the volumes thus far issued. Others **are** in preparation.

THE CAUSE OF AN ICE AGE. By Sir ROBERT BALL, LL. D., F. R. S., Royal Astronomer of Ireland, author of "Starland." 12mo. Cloth, $1.00.

"Sir Robert Ball's book is, as a matter of course, admirably written. Though but a small one, it is a most important contribution to geology."—*London Saturday Review.*

"A fascinating subject, cleverly related and almost colloquially discussed."—*Philadelphia Public Ledger.*

THE HORSE: A Study in Natural History. By WILLIAM H. FLOWER, C. B., Director in the British Natural History Museum. With 27 Illustrations. 12mo. Cloth, $1.00.

"The author admits that there are 3,800 separate treatises on the horse already published, but he thinks that he can add something to the amount of useful information new before the public, and that something not heretofore written will be found in this book. The volume gives a large amount of information, both scientific and practical, on the noble animal of which it treats."—*New York Commercial Advertiser.*

"A study in natural history that every one who has anything to do with the most useful of animals should possess. The whole anatomy is very fully described and illustrated."—*Philadelphia Bulletin.*

THE OAK: A Study in Botany. By H. MARSHALL WARD, F. R. S. With 53 Illustrations. 12mo. Cloth, $1.00.

"An excellent volume for young persons with a taste for scientific studies, because it will lead them from the contemplation of superficial appearances and those generalities which are so misleading to the immature mind, to a consideration of the methods of systematic investigation."—*Boston Beacon.*

"From the acorn to the timber which has figured so gloriously in English ships and houses, the tree is fully described, and all its living and preserved beauties and virtues, in nature and in construction, are recounted and pictured."—*Brooklyn Eagle.*

ETHNOLOGY IN FOLKLORE. By GEORGE LAWRENCE GOMME, F. S. A., President of the Folklore Society, etc. 12mo. Cloth, $1.00.

New York: D. APPLETON & CO., 1, 3, & 5 Bond Street.

In preparation.

MAN AND THE STATE:

STUDIES IN APPLIED SOCIOLOGY.

LECTURES AND DISCUSSIONS BEFORE THE BROOKLYN ETHICAL ASSOCIATION.

CONTENTS.

☞ SEPARATE LECTURES, in pamphlet form, issued fortnightly, price, $0 10
Bound volume, cloth, with index . . . . " 2 00

D. APPLETON & CO., Publishers, 1, 3, & 5 Bond Street, New York.

www.ingramcontent.com/pod-product-compliance
Lightning Source LLC
Chambersburg PA
CBHW021540270326

41930CB00008B/1313